Scotland in Film

Scotland in Film

Forsyth Hardy

EDINBURGH UNIVERSITY PRESS

791. 4362411

© Forsyth Hardy 1990
Edinburgh University Press
22 George Square, Edinburgh

Set in Palatino
on the Telos Text Composition System
and printed in Great Britain by
The Alden Press Limited, Oxford

British Library Cataloguing
in Publication Data
Hardy, Forsyth
Scotland in Film
1. Cinema films. Special subjects: Scotland
I. Title
791.4362411

493608

ISBN   0 7486 0160 0
       0 7486 0183 X pbk

The publisher acknowledges subsidy from
the Scottish Arts Council towards
the publication of this volume

Contents

Acknowledgements

I would like to acknowledge the help of the Scottish Arts Council who gave me a grant at an early stage of my research. The National Film Archive kindly arranged for me to view several Scottish films not normally available. The British Film Institute supplied stills from its collection and provided production details for some of the films. I was able to draw on stills from films of Scotland productions now in the care of the Curator of the Scottish Film Archive. Others came from the collection of the Edinburgh Film Guild at Filmhouse.

I am grateful to Neil Paterson for welcoming the idea of the book and for reading the chapter on the work of the Films of Scotland Committee, even if he found it 'deliberately modest and low key'. Jim Hickey, Director of the Edinburgh Filmhouse, read the concluding chapters and made helpful suggestions. Another reader of the typescript was understandably pleased 'to be reminded how witty and and apposite practically everything Grierson said still seems to be'. M. F. was a constant source of encouragement during the months of research and the writing of the book.

I would like to thank the film production companies, both past and present, whose film stills appear in these pages:
Metro-Goldwyn-Mayer, Paramount, Rock Studios, London Films, Gaumont-British, Radio Pictures, 20th Century-Fox, Scottish Television, Empire Marketing Board Film Unit, General Post Office Film Unit, Film Centre, Paul Rotha Productions, Greenpark, The Archers, Gainsborough Studios, Ealing Studios, Nolbandov-Parkyn Productions, British Film Institute Production Board, Columbia-EMI-Warner, 7.84 Theatre Company, Umbrella Films, Portman Productions, Evarallin, Antonine Productions, Highlander Productions, Scottish Film Production Fund, Oscar Marzaroli.

Forsyth Hardy
Edinburgh 1990

Preface

SIR DENIS FORMAN

Forsyth Hardy is the only person who could have written *Scotland in Film*. Others could have collected the facts, looked up reviews and formed retrospective opinions. But he alone can give us a first-hand account of the circumstances surrounding almost every film made in Scotland over a span of some 50 years.

He was often a principal in their production, first as the representative of the Scottish Office at the Films Division of the Ministry of Information (later the C.O.I.) when it was his duty to initiate and bring to life each film, then to shepherd it through the English bureaucracy, who had no special interest in things Scottish. I can recall seeing him wince at the mispronunciation of simple place names such as Kirkcudbright or Ecclefechan. He was again a prime mover in the setting up and in the direction of Films of Scotland and his account of this period in his career is by any standard far too modest. One could truthfully say that Forsyth Hardy, as well as being the standard bearer for the Scottish documentary, was also both the staff officer and the field commander who fought them through to the screen. Certainly he has instigated more Scottish films than any other living Scotsman.

Along with Norman Wilson he was the author and organiser of the Edinburgh Film Festival which provided an ideal showcase in which Scottish-made films could be seen by an international audience. The festival itself attracted films from all over the globe and therefore film makers as illustrious as Orson Welles, Robert Flaherty, Max Ophuls and John Grierson were drawn to Edinburgh, but it did not escape my notice that despite the competition from international celebrities and their films no Scottish-made film was ever denied a place in the sun.

vii

Quite aside from the great value of this latest book as a work of reference it is a pleasure once again to read Forsyth Hardy's prose. His biography of Grierson and the many articles he has written for *The Scotsman* have always delighted his friends, and once again we can enjoy his very personal style, which consists of an admixture of perceptive criticism, humour and scholarship.

I commend this book not only to the reader who has an interest in films or in Scotland, but also to every library and to every institution in any part of the world where there is a Scottish community which ought to know what their country has achieved in terms of films on the screen.

1
Through Myth to Reality

In the spring of 1953 the Hollywood producer Arthur Freed paid a visit to Scotland. When we met in Edinburgh he told me he wanted to find a village in the Highlands which could look unchanged with its inhabitants just awakened after the passage of a hundred years.

I took him first to Culross on the Firth of Forth, explaining that it was not a Highland village but was certainly very little changed since the seventeenth century. The domestic dwellings with their crow-stepped gables, lintel stones carved with initials, and sun-dials on the corners of the houses were right. We travelled northwards, noting the little houses in Cathedral Street, Dunkeld. Comrie, set against the Grampian foothills on the Highland fault, I thought might give him what he wanted, especially as it had an old hump-backed bridge, necessary for the storyline. Braemar, next on the exploratory journey, had the sought-for Highland ambience. Then a long leap west to Inverary, its shoreline buildings well preserved and enjoying a highly picturesque location on the head of Loch Fyne, which I thought would have an appeal for him. He insisted on seeing Brig-o'-Doon, although I assured him it had nothing to do with the Highlands.

Then Arthur Freed went back to Hollywood and declared: 'I went to Scotland but I could find nothing that looked like Scotland'.

He was, of course, preparing to produce *Brigadoon* which has become the archetypical film of a bogus Scotland. In defence of the producer, who had Vincente Minnelli as director and Gene Kelly and Cyd Charisse in the main roles, it could be said that the story of a magical village which went to sleep in 1754 to wake up for a day each century could never have survived production in a natural setting, even if one could have been found to satisfy Arthur Freed. Alan Jay Lerner did not altogether agree. *Brigadoon*,

1

he wrote in his autobiography, 'was a picture which should have been made on location in Scotland and was done in the studio. It was a singing show that tried to become a dancing show, and it had an all-American cast which should have been all-Scottish. It was one of those ventures that occur so often when we all knew we were going down the wrong road but no one could stop'. But what image of Scotland was in Arthur Freed's mind, and how did it get there?

I have been fascinated by this question, in its general application, ever since I began to write about films in the early thirties, and particularly later, when I was directly involved as a producer of documentaries projecting the life and achievement of Scotland. The popular conception of Scotland appears to be of a wild, mountainous country, picturesque glens, heather-clad moors, with deer on the hills, eagles hovering overhead, and shaggy Highland cattle by the lochside. Kilted Highlanders will be there, gillies driving grouse towards sportsmen in hides, and above all, the sound of pipes. Abandoned castles on islands in lochs, forbidding keeps in the borderland, once-great abbeys in ruins. Perhaps Georgian Edinburgh. Perhaps granite Aberdeen. Everything in strong colour, except when wrapped in mist.

To this picture many influences have contributed. At one period, and certainly for a long time, the strongest was literature. In his ballads and novels, Sir Walter Scott gave the world his own romantic conception of

> Caledonia stern and wild,
> Meet nurse for a poetic child!
> Land of brown heath and shaggy wood,
> Land of the mountain and the flood.

Scott's novels are still required reading in many European schools, as well as in English-speaking countries throughout the world. Some remarkable examples of his influence were given at a conference on Scott held in Canada in 1987. One contributor showed how Scott's popularity on the U. S. frontier influenced not only the fictional shapes of the Wild West novel and film, but also the actual behaviour of real cowboys. It was revealed that *The Lady of the Lake* was translated into the Mohawk tongue as early as 1814, when the

1. Gene Kelly in Vincente Minnelli's *Brigadoon* (1954): the archetypal film of a bogus Scotland.

Indians saw some relationship between the Gaelic clan society and their own way of life. In Eastern Europe Scott was hailed as the first historical realist in fiction. He made a considerable impact on Russia through Pushkin. Scott influenced nineteenth-century painting through his scenic descriptions and his projections of real and imagined conflicts in Scottish history. His interpretation of the Scottish story was perpetuated in the many films made of his novels.

Stevenson is almost always linked with Scott when visitors speak about their preconceptions of the country. The many versions of *Kidnapped* alone must have reinforced Scott's picture of a land where swashbuckling adventure abounded. Add to Scott and Stevenson the poems of Burns and the plays of Barrie, and we have the mainstream influences from literature.

The wild romantic image was supported by the artists. Horatio McCulloch's landscapes, endlessly reproduced, must have spread a misleadingly limited picture far and wide, while Sir Edwin Landseer presented Scotland in terms of stag and steer on misty purple mountainsides and for domestic studies there were the paintings of David Allan and Sir David Wilkie.

Indirectly, by courtesy of Shakespeare, we have from history *Macbeth* with its picture of murder and mayhem and other dark deeds at dead of night. The troubled story of Mary Stuart has been told endlessly in books, on the stage and on the screen, and she must be the historical character most firmly established wherever even a little is known about Scotland. Her only contestant would be Prince Charles Edward Stuart whose image as the embodiment of youthful idealism has become in modern times a little tarnished.

One other image source is the Scot of the music hall. It has been said of Sir Harry Lauder and his successors that they travestied the nation, making a kind of comic strip of Scotland. Widely popular in the twenties and thirties at home and overseas, the picture had some elements of truth or it would never have been accepted anywhere. But by many Scots who think differently about their native country it has been strongly resented as a caricature, a reaction once well expressed by John Grierson:

> The synthetic picture of kilties and comics hurts when a nation remembers that it has been in its time both Robinson Crusoe

and Paul Jones, conquered large slabs of Russia for the Czars, been so eager to fight out the fate of Canada that it provided warriors for both armies at Quebec, emancipated a couple of South American countries, developed steam and steamhammers and bridge-building and shipbuilding and Macadam road-building and modern surgery, founded logarithms and the Bank of England, and travelled first down the big rivers of Africa and across Canada and Australia and, as the map will testify, many other places as well.

I shall be concerned here primarily with what the film has done, to portray or misrepresent or exploit. All has not been to the detriment of Scotland and the Scot. For a small country – smaller than any of the American States, smaller than Norway and Denmark – Scotland has had a sizeable screen presence, even if most of the films have been the result of initiatives from outside the country. Some at least of these approaches by Englishmen and Americans have been genuine efforts to achieve authentic and credible portrayal.

In the face of the outspoken condemnation of *Brigadoon* in Scotland, Arthur Freed might well have said: 'If you think its picture of Scotland is farcically absurd, why don't you put something better in its place?' An answer involves more than a simple desire to meet the challenge. It is too easy to be negative and condemn the caricature. What kind of Scotland do we wish to project? It should not be backward-looking, drawing on history and the written word. It should be about the here and now, the lives of people in the town and the countryside. It cannot always be a cheerful picture, given the economic decline of the country; but if it catches the infinite warmth of the Scottish streets and the people of the Scottish countryside it can still be positive. Albert Finney said not so long ago that he found a pulse, an energy, about Glasgow that he loved. Some film-makers have begun to find that, and others may become aware of vitality in other parts of Scotland – even in Edinburgh, where a little amateur film called *The Singing Street* came near to the bone of the Scottish character.

Have we the means to achieve a Scottish cinema? Ian Macpherson, who wrote so perceptively about Highland village life, once said

2. Frederic March as Mr Hyde in Rouben Mamoulian's version of *Dr. Jekyll and Mr Hyde* (1932).

3.   The race up the cliff on Foula in Michael Powell's *The Edge of the World*
     (1937): concerned with death from its opening sequence, the film ends
     with the unrelenting Elder falling to his death from the clifftop rather
     than leaving with the others.

that 'if films were steam-driven I am sure we should be making very good ones in Scotland by now'. He thought they had not commended themselves to the Scottish genius. Perhaps he had a point. Perhaps in the arts in Scotland words have always been stronger than pictures and Scottish imaginative expression has found an outlet most often in books. That, I believe, is changing as the opportunities offered by film and television are appreciated and the two media, once so strenuously separated, are increasingly coming together.

In suggesting a path through the myths to reality I believe it will be worthwhile to recall some of the attempts to portray Scotland on the screen. That is what I have sought to do in this book.

2
From Annie Laurie to the Glourie

The first film I recall seeing about Scotland was *Annie Laurie* (1927). Produced in Hollywood, this somehow contrived to combine a romantic story about the heroine commemorated in the Burns song with, of all things, the Massacre of Glencoe. In the film Annie Laurie is in love with a MacDonald and her mission, to persuade the Clan Chief to sign a treaty which might have prevented the massacre, fails. Already the film found the road to travesty the easiest one to follow. A contemporary review spoke about 'the very regrettable affair' at Glencoe, of the participation of a heroine in 'incidents which occurred some years before she was born' and of her being serenaded by 'a song which was composed some years after her death'. The writer indicated the spirit in which the film might be approached: 'There are cattle raids in moonlit glens, Highland reels and the tossing of cabers and cutting of capers, any amount of bagpipes and armed clansmen, and the massacre is carried out according to plan, with blackest treachery and superhuman bouts of courage and physical strength'. It might have been a kind of warning of things to come.

Annie Laurie was played by Lillian Gish – but the director was John S. Robertson and not the mighty D. W. Griffith, or the result might have been somewhat different. In her autobiography, *The Movies, Mr. Griffith and Me*, she wrote that 'films should, wherever possible, be made in the actual location of their stories'. That did not happen with *Annie Laurie*. Lillian Gish herself, acknowledging that the heroine lacked emotional depth and stature, dismissed it in a sentence. 'Fans always wrote asking why I didn't smile more often in films; I did in *Annie Laurie* but I don't recall that it helped much'.

Perhaps it was inevitable that the earliest films should seize on the familiar characters and the well-known symbols. *The Loves*

9

of Robert Burns (1930) had Joseph Hislop, the Scottish tenor of international reputation, singing such songs as 'Flow Gently, Sweet Afton', 'Comin' Thro' the Rye' and 'Auld Lang Syne'. The film was more a display of his considerable art as a singer than any attempt at biography. As one of the earliest British sound films ('synchronised', as the Censor's certificate had it) the clarity of the recording was remarkable. For the rest, it moved at a slow pace from one staged episode to another. A scene in the kirk of the denunciation and humiliation of Burns and another of a Hogmanay party at the old ale-house at Mauchline had some vitality, but otherwise Herbert Wilcox did not succeed in giving the film movement or momentum. It failed at the box-office, being taken off after a week at the Tivoli in London and in Edinburgh being received with laughter when it opened the city's newest supercinema, the Rutland, in April 1930.

There was more reality in *The Flying Scotsman* (1930) which emerged from John Maxwell's Elstree and had Moore Marriott as the engine driver, so natural that you almost accepted the nonsense in which he was involved. *The Secret of the Loch* (1934) had Seymour Hicks as a scientist trying to persuade London journalists at Invermoriston that the Loch Ness Monster was half brontosaurus, half diplodocus, hatched from a prehistoric egg preserved from decay in the unplumbed waters of the loch – as good a theory as any today.

Wedding Group (1933), directed by Alex Bryce, gave Alastair Sim one of his earliest parts – as a stern Scottish minister at the time of the Crimean War. Sim had spent some years in Edinburgh teaching young men preparing for the pulpit how to speak, so he came to the film with an inside knowledge. When the setting for the romantic story moved to the Crimea, with a rewarding part for Fay Compton as Florence Nightingale, Sim was less in evidence, but he had shown enough confidence on the screen to secure other parts, including the crotchety news editor in *This Man is News* (1937), written by the Glasgow journalists Roger Macdougall and Allan Mackinnon, and directed with a flair for well-timed and fast-moving action by another Scot, David Macdonald.

With *Red Ensign* (1934) we begin to have a Scottish subject taken a little more seriously. This was Michael Powell's introduction to

4. Michael Powell about 1950: he regarded *The Edge of the World* as a turning-point in his life, and was to return to Scotland more than once.

Scotland, although apart from a symbolic aerial shot of the delayed Cunarder on the stocks at Clydebank, the film and its director were studio-bound. Powell already had the idea of his St Kilda film, *The Edge of the World*, in his mind but was still working his movie apprenticeship by making quota quickies (British films cheaply produced to satisfy the requirements of film legislation). In *Red Ensign* Leslie Banks had the part of a Glasgow shipbuilder determined to build a new type of cargo carrier to bring work and prosperity to the Clyde. Powell thought of it as a semi-documentary with a serious social theme. Hampered by its miniscule budget and studio shooting, it still made an impact through the quality of the direction and sincerity of the actors, including John Laurie, who was to appear regularly in Powell's films. It also marked, modestly, the beginning of Powell's association with Alfred Junge, the art director, who had been trained at the Berlin UFA studios and who was to become a valued member of Powell's creative team.

The idea of *Red Ensign* came from a newspaper article, and the treatment was written by Powell. So also was the case with *The Edge of the World* (1936-37). Powell carried with him for some six years a cutting from *The Observer* describing the evacuation in 1930 of St Kilda. In the conflict between a savage little group of islands west of the Hebrides, their thousand-foot cliffs defying the Atlantic storms, and a small community of men and women, isolated from the mainland for long periods and struggling against the elements to live off sheep and the seabirds, he found a challenging theme. Its production was as fraught with problems as anything the islanders had to face.

Never having been in Scotland, Powell wrote his story in advance, reading everything he could find about the Hebrides, including a book by Alastair Alpin MacGregor, *The Last Days of St Kilda*, based on the author's experiences on the island where he spent the last six months before the evacuation. Powell tried to sell the idea to many producers but at a time when the main source for British films was the London West End stage they would have none of it. Eventually he found a small-time Hollywood producer, Joe Rock, who, having made *Krakatoa* on a volcanic outcrop in the South Pacific, was interested in island subjects. He agreed to back the film. After

12

other preparations and casting, Powell set out for Scotland to see the Earl of Dumfries, the owner of the island group. He was adamant in refusing permission for any film company to land on St Kilda. He had bought the island as a bird sanctuary and the birds must not be disturbed. Powell was dismayed. He had sold the idea to Joe Rock on the basis of filming on St Kilda.

When I first met Michael Powell in the office of *The Scotsman* (I was the newspaper's first film critic) he was in a state of shock. He had to find an alternative island before returning to London or he would lose his finance for the film. It was suggested he should see John Mathieson, secretary of the Royal Scottish Geographical Society, and out of this meeting came the proposal to use Foula, off the Shetland Islands, almost as isolated as St Kilda and with equally precipitous cliffs, home of thousands of seabirds. It had the advantage, from the film-makers' point of view, of having a small population which meant that there would be 'islanders' to augment the film's cast. It also meant some easing – but not much – of communication problems.

The substitution of Foula for St Kilda meant that what Powell had written about a Gaelic-speaking island had now to be adapted to one where Norse was an important influence. I remember finding him in his Edinburgh hotel working hard on the revision of the script. However, the basic theme of the gradual evacuation of the outer islands was common to both St Kilda and (as at least a threat) Foula. It was as far away as it could be from the West End play and the pursuit of the artificial. This may not seem to be a virtue of much consequence today when cameras can penetrate everywhere and films have largely deserted the studios; but it was exceptional in 1936 when critics were still protesting that anywhere outside London was ignored by British film-makers.

This is not to suggest that *The Edge of the World* was a documentary. Powell was indignant when it was suggested to him that he was going to make something like Flaherty's *Man of Aran* or Leon Poirier's *Pêcheur d'Islande*. His film had its origin in reality and drew its strength from its natural location. What Powell added – as he did in all his films – was an imaginative conception. He was concerned with death, from the opening of the film, where a young islander

13

returns after ten years to find it ghostly with the memories of those who were driven from its shores, to the symbolism at the end as the unrelenting Elder falls to his death from the cliff top rather than leave with the others.

Writing many years after the production of the film, and perhaps reading into it more than Powell intended, the critic Kevin Gough-Yates said:

Dominating the conception of the film is the power of the imagination to transform the unacceptable into a more palatable form. The sermon which warns against attributing influence to the supernatural, when events conflict with expectation and hope, finds its echo in Peter Manson's belief that the elements influence human action. Powell's use of the sounds of squalling gulls, the violent storms, the primitive duel to solve a conflict of reason, and screaming music to announce death, invites the possibility that natural events can be attributed to the gods. The islanders, who know that a clear view of the hills of Scotland is an ill omen, accept their fate passively.

At the time I admit, I did not think of the film in these terms. In Scotland we were grateful to have at last a film which owed nothing to the kilties and the comics and could also be assessed as a valid contribution to the cinema. The progress of the film on Foula between June and October 1936 was keenly followed. Powell had to cope with the eccentric weather patterns of Foula, where the light was never consistent and could change in minutes as storms blew in from the south-west. Nevertheless he stuck tenaciously to his task and inspired actors and technicians to do likewise. Out of their shared experiences were to grow lasting friendships. The names of technicians and actors used on this film were to reappear in the credits of much of Powell's later work.

The director's own estimation of his film is worth quoting, especially in the context of this book: 'When a theme has beauty, integrity and a national as well as human experience, it is apt to last a long time, even in such a brittle and ephemeral shape as eight cans of celluloid; and when you add the spirit of an old land and its

P·2-117.

5. Conrad Veidt in Powell and Pressburger's *The Spy in Black* (1939): a
    U-Boat commander enters Scapa Flow in order to sink the British
    fleet, strangely prophetic, but never as important a film as *The Edge
    of the World.*

people, strong enough to influence the shaping of a theme, you have something more'.

Powell regarded *The Edge of the World* as a turning-point in his life. He found it impossible to return to the kind of films he had been making. It also brought him back to Scotland more than once, and helped to give him a warm affection for the country.

It was not long before Powell was back in Scotland, in 1939 preparing to make *The Spy in Black* in the Orkney Islands. The title and the location came from a novel by J. Storer Clouston whose story had been rewritten by Emeric Pressburger – the beginning of a long and fruitful association between director and writer. As a result of the success of *The Edge of the World* Powell was now under contract to Alexander Korda who wanted a 'vehicle' for two of his stars, Conrad Veidt (who symbolised all that was memorable in the Golden Period of the German cinema) and Valerie Hobson. In Pressburger's version 'the spy in black' became a U-boat commander who entered Scapa Flow to sink half of the British fleet (a grim pre-vision of what was to happen).

This was never to be as important a film for Powell, or for Scotland, as *The Edge of the World*. Powell was able to visit Orkney, to see Scapa Flow, to cross from Stromness to 'the great humpy island of Hoy' and to look down on the Old Man, the stack which is completely detached from the adjoining high cliffs. The director was determined to use it as the secret landing point for the U-boat commander. A limited budget made a Foula exercise impossible and, apart from atmospheric establishing shots, the film was made at Denham. It succeeded as a thriller but did not add much to the filmed story of Scotland

In his autobiography *A Life in the Movies*, Powell writes of having become a lover of Scotland even although he did not cross the border until he was thirty. Contributing to the conquest, he says, were Walter Scott, Robert Louis Stevenson, Robert Burns and John Buchan, 'all great tale-spinners and subtle propagandists for their mother country'.

As a tale-spinner John Buchan contributed less to the cinema than we might have expected. *The Thirty-Nine Steps* (1935) remains the best known example, more by virtue of the direction of Alfred Hitchcock than of Buchan's authorship. When I first saw the film I reacted disproportionately to a sequence set in a Highland crofter's cottage which seemed to underline the charge of meanness so often brought against Scots. Much later I came across a passage in an exhaustive study of Hitchcock, *The Murderous Gaze*, by an American professor, William Rothman, which suggested that the reaction was at least relevant: 'The crofter, John, is short of words, crafty, always thinking of ways of squeezing an extra penny's profit, puritanical, and suspicious, particularly of Englishmen. A stereotype of the Scotsman, he adds local colour . . . ' A tribute of a kind to John Laurie, to be able to convey so much in so short a sequence, shared with Peggy Ashcroft as the crofter's mis-matched wife.

As for the film, it did not say very much about Scotland, although Hitchcock made of it a fast-moving, exciting thriller, with a notably dramatic sequence on a train crossing the Forth rail bridge. The director told the story of Richard Hannay's adventures with a fine relish, retaining the spirit if not the letter of the novel. Much of the appeal of the film lay in Robert Donat's performance, with its good humour and pleasant informality, while Madeleine Carroll responded with spirit to the situation in which she is handcuffed to a man she detests. Godfrey Tearle played the spy-villain and Wylie Watson the Memory Man who gives away the secret because professionally he cannot lie.

I had met Hitchcock at Elstree when he was between *Blackmail* (1929) and *Rich and Strange* (1932) and was to meet him again on several occasions when he was making his British thrillers, once memorably on the set of *Sabotage* at the Lime Grove Studios for the key scene in which Sylvia Sydney walks round the kitchen table and plunges a carving knife into the back of Oscar Homolka. I could not persuade the director to locate any other films in Scotland. He preferred the metropolitan scene, more productive of the sinister and the sensational.

Hitchcock, still working in Britain, found something to praise in *Storm in a Teacup* (1937) because it made refreshing contact with 'that vital central stratum of British humanity, the middle class'. In accordance with the fashion of the period it came from the

6. Madeleine Carroll and Robert Donat in Alfred Hitchcock's *The Thirty-Nine Steps* (1935): it did not say much about Scotland, though Hitchcock made of it a fast-moving, exciting thriller.

(© Gaumont)

7.   Katharine Hepburn in John Ford's *Mary of Scotland* (1936): Hepburn's strident, hoydenish Mary did not suggest for a moment someone brought up at the court of Henry II and Catherine de Medici.

theatre – an adaptation by James Bridie of a play by Bruno Frank. Bridie had cleverly transposed the play to a small Scottish town and had worked into it his feeling for Scottish character and his flair for spontaneous humorous detail.

The people Hitchcock identified as 'middle class' were the swollen-headed provost of the town, preoccupied with political ambition and irritated by a poor woman fussing over her dog; a quixotic young journalist obstinately fond of justice; the provost's daughter, torn between natural affection for her father and love for the journalist leading the campaign against him; and the poor woman who cannot afford the licence for her mongrel. Comparatively ordinary people whose lives made appealing drama because they were simple, honest and recognisable. The direction of the film was shared between the experienced Victor Saville and the Scot, Ian Dalrymple, who, with Bridie, ensured the authenticity of the Scottish setting. They also drew convincing performances from the players – Rex Harrison, Vivien Leigh, Cecil Parker, Gus McNaughton, Ursula Jeans and Sara Allgood. A charming little film which did no disservice to Scotland.

Several of Bridie's plays were later brought to the screen. It was the cinema's and Scotland's loss, that he was not persuaded to express his ideas directly in film form and that the adaptations had an inevitable theatricality. How good a film about a genuine facet of Scottish life could have been made, for example, of the idea embodied in *Mr Gillie* – a dominie of the old school who nurtures the creative spark wherever he finds it and who preaches the poverty of richness and the wealth of the imagination. It could have made a film of the order of *Mr Chips* – and there was Alastair Sim to make of it a character study of real depth. One of the saddest of lost opportunities.

In the thirties, plays of proved popularity very often became films. Ready-made plots and dialogue and the reputation of the authors were magnets which the studios, with hungry, demanding production schedules to fill, found it difficult to resist. J. M. Barrie's plays were well-known in the United States by the time the cinema acquired sound. Charles Frohman produced *The Little Minister* on

From Annie Laurie to the Glourie

Broadway as early as 1897 and *What Every Woman Knows* in 1908, both starring Maude Adams. Even before the coming of sound there were two versions of *The Little Minister*, both released in 1921 – the Vitagraph film starring Alice Calhoun and Jimmy Morrison and the one made, more elaborately, by Paramount starring Betty Compson and George Hackathorne. Neither was as successful in drawing audiences as the stage productions with Maude Adams.

Time has not dealt kindly with Barrie's reputation. Fairy-tale and whimsy have long been out of fashion and ears are not attuned to 'the horns of elf-land gently blowing'. It requires a considerable effort therefore to find virtue in the versions of *What Every Woman Knows* and *The Little Minister* made in 1934 which even at the time of their production must have appeared to present a deplorably maudlin image of the Scot. In a letter to Henry James, Stevenson once wrote of Barrie that 'there was genius in him, but there was a journalist at his elbow'. Barrie based his characters on observation of his contemporaries and introduced to audiences outside Scotland unfamiliar aspects of the country. Sometimes they were just too unfamiliar. What did they make in downtown Chicago of the rivalry between the Auld Lichts and the U.P.s in *The Little Minister*?

The theme of *What Every Woman Knows* – that behind every successful man is a woman more perceptive and with greater resources – has a certain universality. Barrie's particular illustration of it took the form of a bargain made by the family of a supposedly unattractive young woman that she shall legally marry a young man with political ambitions who, when he is successful in Parliament, fails to realise the source of his success. In its essentials the film was faithful to the original, although the four-act structure of the stage version was broken up to provide the film with greater variety in its background. In the part created by Maude Adams, Helen Hayes gave an appealing performance and Brian Ahearne was the ambitious politician, blind to his wife's qualities. David Torrence as the father and Donald Crisp and Dudley Digges helped, as they invariably did, to sustain the illusion of a Scottish setting.

The Little Minister was chosen by R.K.O. when the company was looking for a vehicle for Katharine Hepburn after her success in *Little Women*. The actress had doubts about the part and accepted it when she learned that Margaret Sullavan had been approached. 'I didn't really want to play it until I heard that another actress was desperate for the role. Then it became the most important thing in the world that I should get it'. She may also have been influenced by the fact that Lady Babbie had twice been played on the stage by Maude Adams, to whom she was flattered to be compared.

It was not a happy choice for her or the company. The play had been rewritten twice to provide a better part for Maude Adams, and Barrie himself realised that it had become rather painfully manufactured (although it earned £80,000 for him in the first ten years of its production in the United States). He omitted it from the collected edition of his plays, published in 1928.

The story never came to life on the screen. The village of Thrums, supposedly the setting for a battle between the rebellious weavers and the military called in by the mill owners, remained a shadowy place, almost as contrived a setting as the village in *Brigadoon*. Equally unconvincing was the courtship of the little minister by the gypsy girl, due to marry the master of the castle on the hill. There were obscurities and inconsistencies and a fumbled climax. Katharine Hepburn was too strong a personality for Barrie's whimsy to survive, although she all too clearly tried very hard, while John Beal made what he could of the unrewarding part of the little minister. Again Donald Crisp brought some conviction to the acting as the village doctor. The religious intolerance which formed part of the theme fitted, accurately or not, the prevailing conception of the Scottish social scene. The film was a failure on release and Katharine Hepburn became box-office poison (the transforming triumph of *The Philadelphia Story*, though, was not far away).

Katharine Hepburn could trace her ancestry back to James Hepburn, Earl of Bothwell, third husband of Mary, Queen of Scots. This may have influenced her choice of her next Scottish film, *Mary of Scotland* (1936), although she was in all probability attracted to the subject by the Broadway success of Maxwell Anderson's play, starring Helen Hayes as Mary and Fredric March as Bothwell. She wanted George Cukor as director but after the failure of her immediately previous film, *Sylvia Scarlett*, which he directed, Pandro

8. Warner Baxter and Freddie Bartholomew in *Kidnapped* (1938): so little
    of Stevenson's original remained that the producers were guilty of
    deception.

(© 20th Century-Fox)

Berman, producer at R.K.O., would not agree and instead contracted John Ford who had directed *The Informer* and was to direct *Stagecoach* and *The Grapes of Wrath*.

It was not a good beginning, bringing together two strong-willed characters. There were reports of fighting, bickering and fussing and if Ford emerged as the victor, it did not follow that his male chauvinist attitude was to the benefit of the film and Katharine Hepburn's interpretation of Mary Stuart. Her strident, hoydenish Mary did not suggest for a moment someone brought up in France at the court of Henry II and Catherine de Medici. She became in the opinion of one critic 'a soft-focused unfairly slandered Madonna of the Scottish moors'. Such historical reconstruction as was attempted was ill-informed, confused and lacking in conviction. There was no dramatic flow in the film. At one moment the story appeared to be emerging as a clash between Mary and Elizabeth, the one shown as a womanly woman and the other as a cold, hard schemer. But enter Bothwell with his kilt, his clan and his Hollywood hero manner and the film became a mere costumed variant of the-guy-and-the-girl-and-who-gets-who, with Darnley, a feeble, foppish figure, a loser from the start.

Bothwell (Fredric March) to Darnley, encountered in a dark corridor at Holyrood: 'Well, Darnley, still hanging around, eh?'

Maxwell Anderson's dialogue in blank verse had, of course, disappeared; but this could hardly have been the substitution he expected.

There was a slim attempt towards the close to revive the conflict between the Queens and, as in the stage version, a sequence was interpolated, showing a fictitious meeting between them at Fotheringay; but as Mary mounted the scaffold, her thoughts were with her loyal lover (historically they were by then divorced) and in her ears 'the ghostly skirling of the bag-pipes playing the war song of the Bothwell clan'.

The story of Mary Stuart, her brief reign rich in high drama and fierce conflict with reverberations far beyond the boundaries of Scotland, had been filmed on a number of occasions before the John Ford-Katharine Hepburn version. The first was made in France as early as 1913, to be followed by another in the same year, produced in the United States by Thomas A. Edison and based on Schiller's play. *The Loves of Mary, Queen of Scots* (1923) was made in Britain, with Holyrood Palace, Edinburgh and Stirling Castles among the settings. There were to be other films in the post-war period, but none has been wholly satisfactory. The subject still stirs the imagination of writers and dramatists, and I shall return to it later.

Hollywood in the 'thirties had not quite finished with Scotland. Still to come was *Kidnapped* (1938). This laid claim to Stevenson as the author, but so little of the original remained that the producers were guilty of deception. The pursuit motif, yielding an abundance of lively and exciting incident, was abandoned, and in its place there was an unlikely and tedious romance between Alan Breck and a certain Jennie Macdonald of Glencoe whose betrothed, James Stewart, has murdered the Red Fox. Odd echoes of the original were heard and David Balfour's visit to the House of Shaws gave the film its most authentic and impressive sequence. But nothing of the fight in the roundhouse, the eventful voyage round Cape Wrath, the wreck on the reef at Mull, the wanderings over the island and across Morven, the flight in the heather, Cluny's cage and the crossing of the Forth at the end of the flight. What a waste of magnificent material! For the record Warner Baxter was called Alan Breck and Freddie Bartholomew David Balfour, while Darryl Zanuck's latest 'discovery', Arleen Whelan, played the imported heroine.

In addition to these, the pre-war decade included several films with tenuous Scottish connections. In *The Ghost Goes West* (1935) the connection with Scotland, however slender, was welcome, if only because it was something entirely different – a sophisticated comedy, directed by a Frenchman. Based on a *Punch* story by Eric Keown, it concerned a feud dating from 1745 between two clans, the Glouries and the MacLaggans, which will end only when a MacLaggan is forced to admit that one Glourie is worth seven of his clan. The ghost is the double of the contemporary Glourie who, in order to pay his debts, sells his castle to an American millionaire who transports it, stone by stone and complete with Ghost, to Florida where a rival business man turns out to be of

25

9. Jean Parker and Robert Donat in René Clair's *The Ghost Goes West* (1935): interestingly and unusually, a sophisticated comedy, directed by a Frenchman, though the Scottish connection is slender.

G. G - 219.

10. John Grierson in 1964: an extraordinarily gifted man, a visionary determined to make a better life for the ordinary citizen.

(courtesy STV)

MacLaggan blood. No one took the story too seriously and the players responded light-heartedly to the mood determined by René Clair – a mood which encompassed comedy, fantasy and sentimental romance. Robert Donat as both the Ghost and his descendant acted with invincible naturalness and Eugene Pallette, magnificently rotund in the kilt, made the American millionaire a likeable figure of fun. I am sure none of the film was shot any nearer the Highlands than Denham Studios but here it did not seem to matter because there was a lively imagination shaping the confection. It had at least one unforgettable moment – the entry into the castle hall of a Negro band, in the kilt, playing Scottish airs.

Said O'Reilly to McNab (1937), a Scots-Irish comedy from the music hall, gave a hint of the quality of Will Fyffe. Noting that the humour was robust rather than subtle, as the acting, John Grierson wrote that 'Fyffe, if encouraged, might easily lose his habit of music hall emphasis and become a good film actor. In one episode, in particular, he becomes gradually and by nuance entangled in a confidence trick, he puts in some quiet and distinguished acting, and shows he has the right idea'. Grierson considered the film as 'taking a further step in the humble development of real British cinema'.

Will Fyffe had a larger opportunity in his next film. *Owd Bob* (1938) was a story of the Cumberland shepherds and their dogs, the annual excitement of the sheep-dog trials and the threat to the community of a dog that runs wild and kills the sheep. Slight and simple, part of the film's appeal lay in the persuasive reality of the Eskdale scene, with its bare landscapes and sullen rain-piled skies, part in the graphically photographed trials, and part in the performance of Will Fyffe as the old shepherd who stumps menacingly about his farm, Bannockburn, and sets his black Alsatian at every man and beast setting foot on it. Fyffe used his experience of the music hall to give range and richness to his study of the cunning, blustering old misanthrope. Moore Marriott and Graham Moffat were there to add to the comedy, Margaret Lockwood and John Loder provided the romance and the film was directed by Robert Stevenson before he went to Hollywood.

Will Fyffe showed more understanding of what he might have given to a Scottish cinema than any of his contemporaries. He once spoke revealingly of the characters he created – the Highland doctor, the Glasgow drunk and the Scots engineer – built up bit by bit, 'tinged with memories of people I have met and have seen . . . I am Scots and I play them as Scots, because they are the people I know best. It's the human quality that counts – the canniness, the kindliness, the braveries, the big hopes and the small fears'. Here was someone whose vision of Scotland owed nothing to the conventional elements and whose feeling for life had warmth and humour. He disappeared too soon from the Scottish scene, but there were echoes of what he might have contributed in Duncan Macrae and Roddy Macmillan.

I ought to make a passing reference at least to *Bonnie Scotland* (1935) with Laurel and Hardy. They were seen as two visitors from the United States in Scotland to collect an inheritance, which turns out to be a snuff-box. They join a Scottish regiment which is posted to India, in the manner of *Lives of a Bengal Lancer*. There were some amusing passages in the early sequences supposedly set in Scotland; but the film began to disintegrate with the introduction of a romantic sub-plot (June Lang and William Janney). James Finlayson, a Scottish actor who appeared in many of their films, helped the fun along with his characteristic displays of frustration. David Torrence, another Scottish actor often called upon to strengthen the 'Scottish' element in films, was also in the cast. The comedians were later to visit Scotland and to appear on the stage of the largest cinema in Edinburgh, the Playhouse; but they did not again attempt a Scottish subject.

The motivation for the making of all the films I have discussed in this chapter did not come from within Scotland. They formed part of the pattern of film-making in London or Hollywood, items in production schedules. They were made because someone somewhere thought that an idea in a novel or play, or a character from history, would result in a film which audiences all over the world would want to see. Only in one or two cases was the country's scenic grandeur an attraction. With few exceptions the films were derided. Not many of the critics attempted to answer Arthur Freed's blunt question: 'Why don't you do something about it yourselves?'

11. *Drifters* (1929): the first British film to match what the Russian directors were doing in selecting and arranging images to make visual drama, in finding its theme in the everyday story of men at work – and made by a Scot.

3
The Debt to Drifters

So far the projection of Scotland, such as it was, had come through the story films. Documentary was to work a change. Here Scotland's stake was proportionately larger because of the pioneering presence of John Grierson who had founded the documentary movement, on his return in 1927 from a three year sojourn in the United States. Apart from his World War II years in Canada, Grierson was to be a positive influence in the Scottish film scene for the rest of his life.

Grierson was an extraordinarily gifted man, a visionary determined to make a better life for the ordinary citizen. He might have been a preacher – and indeed he was in the pulpit in his university student days and in a sense never left it, although he found other means of reaching the public. He was led to the cinema first by his experience in the United States, when Walter Lippmann told him that film rather than the Press was the dominating public influence of the day, and later by the opportunity he seized in London where the Empire Marketing Board was looking for a means of promoting the marketing of Empire products. By such a bizarre route did he come to found a movement which was to make a significant contribution to social change in Britain and much further afield.

I remember well my first meeting with Grierson. I had seen his film of the Scottish herring fleets, *Drifters* (1929) and had written about it. The film had excited and stimulated me, as much for its form as for its content. Here was a film which matched what the Russian directors were doing in selecting and arranging images to make visual drama. Here also was a film which found its theme in the everyday story of men at work. I imagine that the reaction was coloured also by the pleasure in finding that this revolutionary film – because against the background of London West End theatre British film-making in 1929 it was just that – was the work of a Scot.

31

At any rate Grierson had read my review and, on his first visit to Edinburgh, strode into *The Scotsman* office and barked to a frightened receptionist: 'Where's Hardy?' Later his voice, with its Chicago-sharpened cutting edge, shattered the cathedral calm of the reporters' room while he launched, not into protest at anything in the article as his manner and demeanour might have suggested, but into a vivid outline of his projects and plans. No-one else, then or later, was able to describe with half Grierson's pungency and economy in words what the documentary idea stood for.

The choice of the Scottish herring fleets as the subject of his first film was conditioned by a number of circumstances. Grierson had the sea in his blood. Although his father was a headmaster (at Cambusbarron on the outskirts of Stirling) the family had a long connection with lighthouses. Grierson, serving as a telegraphist on mine-sweepers in the Royal Naval Volunteer Reserve in World War I, was familiar with every port and inlet on the Western seaboard and the isles. The Empire Marketing Board wanted a film on the marketing of herring and the idea had the approval of Walter Elliot, chairman of its film committee and, like Grierson, a graduate of Glasgow University. The Financial Secretary to the Treasury, the department which had to approve the project, had written a book on the herring and its effect on the history of Britain (no less!). It was suggested that the author might give some help and advice. Not for the last time did Grierson employ a little discreet flattery to achieve his end.

The film which resulted demonstrated Grierson's conviction that it was not necessary to go to the ends of the earth for a drama of reality. It was waiting on the doorstep if the film-makers had the imagination to see it and the skill to bring it to the screen. *Drifters* was Grierson's first film – conceived, directed, edited and partly photographed, very much a personal achievement. It was 'rapturously received by the sophisticated audience' at its Film Society showing in London on November 10, 1929, and within a month was in the public cinemas.

In his leadership of the documentary film movement in the 'thirties Grierson ensured that whenever possible the cameras looked northwards. *Drifters* was followed by a group of six short films, two of which were located in Scotland. Basil Wright, the first of the young film-makers to join Grierson at the E.M.B., directed *O'er Hill and Dale* (1930) on Walter Elliot's sheep farm in the Borders, and its lyrical use of landscape gave an early hint of the visual poetry which was to characterise his work. Arthur Elton went to Sutherland to make a film about salmon fishing, *Upstream* (1930) and, while waiting to catch on film the salmon leaping the Falls of Shin, created consternation in budget-conscious Whitehall by sending back reels of salmonless negative. Grierson himself directed a short film *Granton Trawler* (1934), made on a rough voyage on the *Isabella Greig* out of Leith and handed it for editing to Edgar Anstey, another of the socially-conscious young film-makers brought into the E.M.B. unit. A very small beginning for the projection of Scotland, but one firmly based on the lives of real people, not theatrical confections.

The Empire Marketing Board, Grierson considered, 'was a fine chance to make films of ordinary people and the dignities of life in our time. Taking that line, we could have gone on for ever, bringing alive to each other the members of our Commonwealth of Nations. The materials were young, dramatic and inexhaustible. With imagination enough, machinery and support enough, one could, on such a commission, have sighted the eyes and established the sentiments of a generation'.

But that particular road for documentary closed with the disbanding of the E.M.B. in September, 1933. The approach had been explored and the explorers had had their first taste of film-making. *Drifters* apart, the impact was still moderate in scale.

Happily Sir Stephen Tallents, invited to join the staff of the Post Office, was able to take Grierson and the film unit with him from the E.M.B., and the continuity of the movement was assured. Grierson welcomed it, 'for the story of communications was as good as any other and in one sense it was better . . . we had at least the assurance of imaginative backing'.

In the next five years Grierson was to push the communications theme to its uttermost limit. The documentary story could have taken a different course if the unit he had created could have become a common service to all the Government departments.

12. *Night Mail* (1936): as much about loneliness and companionship as about the collection and delivery of letters.

13. Stuart Legg and Donald Alexander's *Wealth of a Nation* (1938): the first product of the Films of Scotland committee.

That all-embracing objective Grierson was not to realise until, in war-time, he founded the National Film Board of Canada.

Two of the films made by the G.P.O. Film Unit are relevant to the subject of this book. One was the documentary classic *Night Mail* (1936). This began humbly enough as an account of the travelling Post Office, the trains which, overnight, travel in both directions between London and Scotland, collecting and delivering bags of mail *en route*. Perhaps because steam-driven trains have a particular attraction for film-makers, the subject fired the imagination of all the members of the unit which by then included Alberto Cavalcanti with his special interest in the experimental use of sound. Grierson decreed that the journey illustrated should be from south to north. He had in mind from the beginning the significance for Scots of crossing the border, and had a joke about being able to detect a bump on the line. He gave the film to direct to Harry Watt, one of his Scottish recruits, while Basil Wright in the cutting-room watched it grow as it emerged from the skilled hands of the editor, R. Q. McNaughton. It was a truly collaborative work of art.

When Grierson saw the first rough assembly he was conscious of something missing. 'What we haven't got here', he said, 'is anything about the people who are going to get the letters. We have only the machinery of getting letters from one point to another. What about the people who wrote them and the people who get them?' While in Chicago, Grierson had known Carl Sandburg and was familiar with his poetry. In 'The Sins of Kalamazoo' there are a few lines expressing the sentiment he had in mind:

Sweethearts there in Kalamazoo
Go to the general window of the post office
And speak their names and ask for letters
And ask again, 'Are you sure there is nothing for me?
I wish you'd look again – there must be a letter for me.

W. H. Auden, who had joined the unit as a production assistant and had worked with Harry Watt on location, was asked to write verse for the concluding sequences of the film. The lines had to fit the images exactly, and many were impatiently discarded by Watt who had at the same time to coordinate sound effects and the music of Benjamin Britten. Eventually the perfect combination was achieved and *Night Mail* became as much a film about loneliness and companionship as about the collection and delivery of letters:

This is the night mail crossing the border,
Bringing the cheque and the postal order,
Letters for the rich, letters for the poor,
The shop at the corner and the girl next door.
Pulling up Beattock, a steady climb –
The gradient's against her but she's on time.
Past cotton grass and moorland boulder,
Shovelling white steam over her shoulder,
Snorting noisily as she passes
Silent miles of wind-bent grasses;
Birds turn their heads as she approaches,
Stare from the bushes at her blank-faced coaches;
Sheep dogs cannot turn her course,
They slumber on with paws across.
In the farm she passes no one wakes,
But a jug in a bedroom gently shakes.

Dawn freshens, the climb is done.
Down towards Glasgow she descends
Towards the steam tugs, yelping down the glade of cranes
Towards the fields of apparatus, the furnaces
Set on the dark plain like gigantic chessmen.
All Scotland waits for her;
In the dark glens, beside the pale-green sea lochs,
Men long for news.

Letters of thanks, letters from banks,
Letters of joy from the girl and boy,
Receipted bills and invitations,
And timid lovers' declarations,
And gossip, gossip from all the nations,
News circumstantial, news financial,
Letters with holiday snaps to enlarge in
Letters with faces scrawled on the margin.

14. *North Sea* (1938): Harry Watt's documentary of the ship-to-shore radio service.

15. The erection of the balloon barrage in the early days of World War Two: *Squadron 992* (1940).

Letters from uncles, cousins and aunts,
Letters to Scotland from the South of France,
Letters of condolence to Highlands and Lowlands,
Notes from overseas to the Hebrides;
Written on paper of every hue,
The pink, the violet, the white and the blue;
The chatty, the catty, the boring, adoring,
The cold and official and the heart's outpouring,
Clever, stupid, short and long,
The typed and the printed and the spelt all wrong.

Thousands are still asleep
Dreaming of terrifying monsters
Or a friendly tea beside the band at Cranston's or Crawford's;
Asleep in working Glasgow, asleep in well-set Edinburgh,
Asleep in granite Aberdeen.
They continue their dreams
But shall awake soon and long for letters.
And none will hear the postman's knock
Without a quickening of the heart,
For who can bear to feel himself forgotten?

Stuart Legg spoke much of the commentary and the moving culminating passage was spoken by Grierson himself.

Night Mail has stood the test of time as very few other documentaries have. Generations of film-goers all over the world have drawn from it a conception of the Scottish Borderland, the bare rounded Cheviot hills – 'heaped like slaughtered horses' was Auden's too vivid simile, one of his discarded lines. There was some criticism here and there that the film did not concern itself sufficiently with the lives of the postal workers – the ordinary citizen of documentary's professed aim. It was too narrow a criticism of a film which generously met other criteria.

Mainly through the influence of Harry Watt and Cavalcanti, documentary was moving away from didactic statement towards personal dramatisation. *North Sea* (1938) marked a point of arrival. Watt found his subject in the ship-to-shore radio service operated by the Post Office – a lifeline for ships at sea in time of danger. He based his script on the records of the Post Office and the shipping companies, of an elderly coal-burning trawler on a routine voyage, hit during a storm by a freak wave which rolls her over so that the coal in the bunker shifts, giving the vessel a dangerous list and choking the pumps. As a report on this life-and-death situation is going out the aerial is carried away before a location can be given. The film described how, for two days and nights, in frightful weather, the crew struggled to stay alive and eventually, having repaired the aerial, were able to report where they were.

In contrast to the usual disclaimer on studio films, the opening title ran: 'The story of the film, and all the names, characters and incidents mentioned or shown, are entirely authentic. The film reconstructs, as it actually happened, an incident in the life of deep-sea fishermen'.

Watt found his characters at the Labour Exchange in Aberdeen, by sitting with the official on duty and listening to the fishermen applying for jobs. He could very quickly tell from their reactions whether or not they were camera material. 'I was looking for faces and personalities and, by God, I got them. They were a wonderful gang', said Watt. He added Bill Blewitt from his Cornwall film, *The Saving of Bill Blewitt* – a masterstroke, he felt. 'As a fellow fisherman, he explained the madnesses of film-making to the rest as one who had gone through it and survived, and made acting look so easy that they just strolled through it behind him'.

Thus *North Sea* had a solid basis in reality. It was a fitting film to stand beside *Drifters* and *Night Mail*. And it was, in origin and creation, a Scottish achievement. Robert Flaherty called it 'one of the most significant short films that has ever been made . . . real incidents such as *North Sea* must be happening everywhere, every day – incidents that if they were filmed would, as the *North Sea* film does, get right under the skin of this country and its people'.

Something like the real Scotland was beginning to edge its way on to the screen. The initiative still lay elsewhere, even if Scots were creatively involved. But a change was on the way. With the major Empire Exhibition of 1938 scheduled for Glasgow there was an upsurge of national feeling which was to find one outlet in the

16. Pioneers of the Scottish documentary, taken at the 1980 Edinburgh International Film Festival. Left to right: Forsyth Hardy, Harry Watt, Basil Wright, Stuart Legg, Edgar Anstey.

17. Producer-director Frank Lloyd outlines a scene for *Ruler of the Seas* for Margaret Lockwood and Will Fyffe.

appointment of a Films of Scotland Committee, charged with the task of producing a series of films of Scottish life for showing at the exhibition (and, if they were good enough, in the cinemas). Finance (£5,000) was contributed by a Glasgow industrialist, Sir John McTaggart. Alex B. King (later Sir Alex), the leading Scottish independent exhibitor, was a member of the Committee, ensuring the distribution of the films; the Scottish newspapers and the film societies gave the effort their enthusiastic support and at the Scottish Office there was Walter Elliott 'to sit in actively on the making of scripts and bring his dashing imagination to the service of the producer' (Grierson).

Against the massive volume of documentary film-making today, the first products must seem modest. *Wealth of a Nation* (1938), produced by Stuart Legg and directed by Donald Alexander, drew a contrast between the old and the new in industrial Scotland. A contrast between the coal, iron and steel of the Industrial Revolution and the shipyards which made Clydebuilt a guarantee of quality for the world, and the new age which was harnessing water power for electricity, turning from the heavy industries to aluminium, and embarking on the plan for new towns to replace the dereliction of the Lowland concentrations. Some of the conclusions may have been over-optimistic; but it was part of Grierson's film philosophy to accentuate the positive.

In *The Face of Scotland* (1938) Basil Wright set out to answer the question, 'What and why is the Scot?' He began in Roman times and showed how Scotland resisted invasion and, encompassing Calvinism along the way, emerged sturdy, independent and unyieldingly democratic. He reminded us, in Ritchie Calder's words, 'of the Scotland of the meagre meal-poke, which bred philosophers out of half-starved students and made skilled craftsmen out of gillies'. He found his climax, not by setting the Scot on some far and fantastic horizon, but by re-discovering, at a Glasgow football match, vigour and strength in the character of the working man. It was a stimulating film to lead the series.

They Made the Land (1938), directed by Mary Field, owed something in style and treatment to the American film *The River*, which introduced Pare Lorentz to the documentary scene. The story of how the Scottish farmer conquered the wet, dour, peat- and heather-laden land was told in heroic terms. It began in the days of the foot plough (no reconstruction but a contemporary example found on a hill-side at Loch Broom) and described farming progress by ways of drainage, afforestation, new crops, cattle breeding and the reforms coming from the research laboratories. The tempo was quiet and measured, as perhaps fitted the subject, but there was criticism of the recitative of the commentary, which Ritchie Calder found 'a kind of linguistic hiccups, or a surfeit of radishes'.

The subject of *The Children's Story* (1938) was Scottish education. Here Alexander Shaw, recalling the influence of John Knox, described the devotion to learning which was once one of the country's strongest traditions and still survives in pockets here and there. It revealed approaches, new in the thirties, to the equipment of children for modern life, with less emphasis on academic grind. Part of the commentary was spoken by Sir William MacKechnie, the enlightened Secretary of the Scottish Education Department – another indication of the creative involvement of the Scottish Office civil servants.

These were the main films in the series. There were also shorter films of Scottish fisheries, *Sea Food*, and others on *Scotland for Fitness* and *Sport in Scotland*. Later there was a film on Dundee.

Verdicts on the series were favourable. Ritchie Calder thought that the films would 'tell the world of the other side of Scotland, tear away the tartan curtains of romance and show a nation fighting for its existence'. Paul Rotha wrote later that 'the project was, and still is, unique in film history and was successful in every way'. The films were much publicised, the subject of newspaper and radio comment and shown by the film societies at special peformances. The potential importance was taken on board.

An editorial in *World Film News* said:

> The case for Scottish films goes deeper than nationalism. If the special qualities of Scottish life and character are conveyed to the screen in dramatic terms they will represent a welcome addition to British film materials. There is an intensity in the Scottish sense of drama which might come to exercise a

healthy influence on the more namby-pamby agonies of the West End. There is a debunking quality in Scottish humour which might provide a measure of relief from the empty antics of Messrs Walls and Lynn. We suspect that in Scottish village life there is the same wealth of caricature and character which is now the special asset of the French cinema. The only thing we ask is that when Scotland goes south with its movies, it will leave Harry Lauder, J. M. Barrie and Robert Burns behind. We can hardly believe that Harry Lauder is true. Wo do not care whether J. M. Barrie is true or not, for we have had too much of him. As for the truth of Burns no Scotsman would dare to tell it, for fear of his fellow Scots.

But for the war, what had begun so modestly might have grown to encompass larger opportunities. Industrialists had shown an interest in film-making and might have come to show more. The Scottish Office had become involved in the use of the cinema to maintain the national will and benefit the national economy. The men who founded the Films of Scotland Committee were prepared to work hard to realise the aims of the voluntary body. Writers and artists had seen how their ideas could reach the screen. Wherever Scottish participation in the life of Britain was under discussion, access to the cinema formed part of the debate. At no other time I can recall was there so much hope in the air, so much belief in Grierson's vision: 'A first duty is the articulation of Scottish problems to the Scot and the firing of his mind and heart to the need of his generation'.

Grierson's seemingly inexhaustible well of inspiration spilled over into many lives. One was Margaret Tait, graduate of the Rome Film School, whose films included a series in Orkney. I recall viewing them with Grierson in Edinburgh when he made helpful and encouraging assessments. Another was Jenny Brown (Gilbertson) who made films in her native Shetland and who was stimulated by Grierson. Her first film, *A Crofter's Life in Shetland*, had its premiere in Edinburgh in 1932. Later came *Rugged Island*. After the war she made many films in the Arctic, some for television in Canada and Britain. At eighty she could

18. Paul Rotha's *Children of the City* (1944); its success annoyed the Home Office in London, who had opposed the film as running the risk of making heroes out of juvenile delinquents.

still spend a year in a small settlement 900 miles within the Arctic Circle, to bring back a faithful and fascinating record of Eskimo life. She always readily acknowledged her debt to Grierson whose work in the thirties brought so many eager tyros into film-making.

4

The War Years

During the war feature films, in the main and understandably, reflected the conflict in the active zones or on the home front. Among them were *In Which We Serve, The Next of Kin, Waterloo Road* and *The Foreman Went to France* (Gordon Jackson's first film appearance). Scotland was not a location for any of the story films.

A curious and perhaps forgotten exception was *Hatter's Castle* (1941), an adaptation of A. J. Cronin's novel which, in the opinion of many, echoed George Douglas's *The House with the Green Shutters*. So gloom-ridden a story hardly added much fun to cinema-going at a time when gloom was not the most highly prized element in films. Most of the film was shot in the studio, in shadowy settings depicting the mansion on the hill and the local pub. Robert Newton as the hatter dominated the action in an over-blown characterisation and there were parts for Emlyn Williams, James Mason, Deborah Kerr, Beatrice Varley and Enid Stamp-Taylor. Not a film which added much to the projection of Scotland.

Another half-forgotten film of the early war period was *Ruler of the Seas* (1939), the story of the first crossing of the Atlantic by steam. A foreword made it clear that it was 'fiction inspired by fact'. What mattered was that the film suggested the spirit which inspired the pioneers who dreamt of building ships that would sail across the Atlantic by steam and who, with patience and perseverance, made the dream a reality. The film opened, with a flourish, on board the sailing-ship Falcon, racing through the storms to reach Greenock on time. Frank Lloyd, the film's Glasgow-born director, admirably caught the atmosphere of the Clyde port; and he managed with dramatic skill the meeting of the young mate of the Falcon, in revolt against the owner's policy of record runs at all costs, and a shrewd old engineer, fired with the faith that the Atlantic could be

19. *Crofters* (1944): made for the 'Pattern of Britain' series, set in the crofting community of Achriesgill, Sutherland.

20. *Crofters*: strange to have to wait for a war to bring alive on the screen this stern and beautiful corner of Scotland.

crossed by steam. Interest mounted as they decided to collaborate in constructing a new engine. Once the Dog Star, the little coastal steamer in which they are to attempt the Atlantic crossing, was under way, the film gathered momentum and despite bad weather, fuel shortage, threatened mutiny, panicky passengers, and an injury to the engineer, the vessel eventually reached New York Harbour. Will Fyffe eagerly seized his first big film opportunity. His engineer was a man of shrewdness, humour and purpose, and again and again the genuine Scottish note was struck. Douglas Fairbanks made a sympathetic figure of the mate and Margaret Lockwood brought a swish of prim petticoats into the masculine setting.

Many of the short British films were concerned with the war effort or with the situation on the Home Front. Harry Watt made *Squadron 992* (1940) about the erection of a balloon barrage around the Forth Bridge-Rosyth area after the first air raid on the British mainland. It had an exciting simulated battle in the air and a sequence of which the director was particularly proud – intercutting of the aerial battle with shots of a whippet chasing a hare on open moorland, based on the actual experience of two eye-witnesses out walking their dog when the raid began. Watt thought it made the film cinematically worthwhile.

Wartime film-making was the responsibility of the Ministry of Information (whose Films Division became a stimulating place to work in after the appointment of Jack Beddington as its Director). Proposals for films on Scottish subjects came from the Scottish Departments at St. Andrew's House in Edinburgh where I had an overall responsibility for the film programme. Although many of them were humdrum, however necessary (*Clean Milk, Defeat Diphtheria, A Farm is Reclaimed*), several were more ambitious.

Power for the Highlands (1943), about peace-time benefits expected from the work of the newly appointed North of Scotland Hydro-Electric Board, was produced before any of the schemes had even reached the drawing board. Tom Johnston, Scotland's visionary Secretary of State, told me he wanted a film which would influence public opinion in favour of what he intended to do. Paul Rotha was given the film to produce and, as there was so little in Scotland to use as illustration, found a meaningful comparison in the much-admired achievement of the Tennessee Valley Authority. A train speeding northwards through the Highlands was the setting for a conversation between two men of the 51st Highland Division and two men of the United States Army. An optimistic engineer and a gamekeeper suspicious of what hydro-electric development would do for the Highlands gave expression to arguments for and against then rampant in Scotland.

Children of the City (1944), also produced by Paul Rotha, was another forward-looking film. Child crime was on the increase in Scotland and Sir Charles Cunningham, Secretary of the Scottish Home Department, felt that a film might constructively look at causes and solutions. Budge Cooper, the director, examined with sympathy and understanding the cases of three boys whose high-spirited gesture in entering a pawn-broker's shop leads to theft. The film's plea was: 'We must make it as exciting for our children to build the new world as is the present temptation to destroy the world of their parents'.

It was *Dead End Kids* written small but done with honesty and sincerity, using natural backgrounds, mainly in Dundee. Its success annoyed the Home Office in London, who had opposed the film as running the risk of making heroes out of juvenile delinquents – but who proceeded to make a similar film of their own about England, *Children on Trial*, much more expensive and much less successful.

Highland Doctor (1943) described the work of the Highlands and Islands medical service which used aircraft to reach isolated communities. 'From farmer's cart to air ambulance – a couple of centuries in a few years', remarks the doctor familiar with conditions before and after the reforms were introduced. Much of the film was shot, under Kay Mander's direction, in Lewis and Harris and North Uist and the photography made the most of the Hebridean scene.

From a different source, the British Council, came another film of the Hebrides, *Western Isles* (1942). The British Council had an annual budget for film-making, the results often being nearer the knee-breeches of ceremonial than the dungarees of the working man. *Land of Invention* showed Scotland as the home of a race of adventurers, listing Macadam, Watt, Murdoch, Nasmyth, Graham

21. *North-East Corner* (1944): the unmistakable flavour of the film owed much to John R. Allan's understanding of land and people.

22. *Waverley Steps* (1947): does in part for Edinburgh what *Rhythm of a City, Berlin* and *Menschen an Sonntag* did for Stockholm and Berlin, and what no other film has done for any other British city.

Bell, Telford and Simpson, with a glimpse or two of roads, steam engines, gas lighting, bridges and chloroform. *Royal Mile* was a tour of the Castle, down the High Street to the Palace of Holyroodhouse, with passing references to Robert Bruce, John Knox and Adam Smith.

Western Isles was more ambitious. It was one of the first Technicolor films to be made in Scotland. The cameraman was Jack Cardiff, whose name was later to be on such films as *Western Approaches*, *Black Narcissus* and *The Red Shoes*. It was made in the Outer Hebrides and showed how the islanders, with courage and determination, met the hardships which war added to their precarious existence. Terence Egan Bishop, the director, drew his story from two wartime episodes: the arrival in Harris of a lifeboat of survivors and the feat of a Lewis deckboy in navigating a ship's lifeboat from somewhere in the Atlantic to the mouth of the English channel. The fusion of the two stories, including the boy's fictitious seventeen mile walk across the island to his father's home, was a legitimate dramatic device. The result was a film which stood out from the wartime propaganda plain. The commentary was spoken by Joseph Macleod who, after the war, was to make a brief, brave effort to bring ambitious film-making to Scotland.

Over fifty short films on Scottish subjects were made during the war and immediate post-war periods. Some of them were made by Scottish companies. Stanley Russell's Glasgow-based Scottish Film Productions made such films as *The River Clyde* (1938) from a script by George Blake, the Scottish novelist. In Edinburgh Campbell Harper Productions with Alan Harper as director and Henry Cooper as his assistant made *A Farm is Reclaimed* (1944), *Freedom of Aberfeldy* (1943) and *Seed of Prosperity* (1946). The Polish director, Eugene Cekalski, collaborated with Hans Nieter O'Leary and Jack Cardiff in making *Scottish Mazurka* (1943), an imaginative record of the sojourn of the Polish forces in Scotland.

Two or three of the films were outstanding and stood the test of time. Made for the 'Pattern of Britain' series, *Crofters* (1944) was set in the little crofting community of Achriesgill in North-West Sutherland. Written and directed by Ralph Keene and superbly photographed by Peter Hennessy, the film showed the crofters bringing in their sheep for the clipping from the distant hill pastures. The picture of everyday life in this stern and beautiful country was rounded out with impressions of peat cutting, gillieing and the hay harvest. Strange to have to wait for a war to bring alive on the screen this distinctive and beguiling little corner of Scotland.

For the same series and again with Ralph Keene in charge was *North-East Corner* (1944), with a script by Aberdeenshire author John R. Allan and Laurie Lee. It moved inland from the little fishing villages round the coast to show how the farms stood on made land, won from the stony hillsides and hungry moors. Pictorially the film was particularly impressive: small boats breasting the waves at the harbour bar matched by shots of neat orderly fields and solid stone-built farmhouses. The unmistakable flavour of the film owed much to John R. Allan's understanding of land and people.

John Eldridge, who directed this film, was also director of *Waverley Steps* (1947), the last Scottish film to be made before the Government ended official participation in film-making. In many ways it was an exceptional film. While at the Scottish Office I had had an ambition to make a film about Edinburgh as different as possible from the tourist travelogues. In Stockholm, researching a book on the Scandinavian cinema, I had seen the work of Arne Sucksdorff and was especially attracted by his *Rhythm of a City*. I brought a copy back with me and showed it to Eldridge and his colleagues at Greenpark, the production company. A treatment written by John Sommerfield was produced which showed the Sucksdorff influence but went beyond that in identifying characters and finding a linking story. It did not make any plea or embody a propaganda point and in a sense there was very little justification for it to be financed by the Government. By happy chance the Secretary of the Scottish Home Department, Sir Charles Cunningham, was not only an enlightened civil servant but also something of a film buff (a founder member of the Edinburgh Film Guild). He saw in embryo what he thought could become an attractive film and gave his approval. Sadie Aitken of the Gateway Theatre helped to guide the director to amateur players in Edinburgh who formed the cast. The director insisted on authentic settings – the Medical School, the

23. Roger Livesey and Wendy Hiller in Powell and Pressburger's *I Know Where I'm Going* (1945): not the stark reality of the deserted St Kilda but a gentle piece of imagined romance, touched by the strangeness of Hebridean myth, and wildly dramatic when it needed to be.

New Club, Moray Place, Leith Docks, St Giles Cathedral – which involved sometimes delicate negotiations but which helped to give the film its character.

As I stand a little too closely to the film for impartial judgment, let me quote the verdict of Richard Winnington, the sharply perceptive critic of the *News Chronicle*, writing about the film when it was shown at the Edinburgh Film Festival:

> *Waverley Steps* does in part for Edinburgh what *Rhythm of a City, Berlin* and *Menschen an Sonntag* did for Stockholm and Berlin, and what no film has done for any other British city. The film was made for the Scottish Office by Greenpark Productions, was written by John Sommerfield, directed by John Eldridge, photographed by Martin Curtis, and is none the worse for the odd dues it pays to those other movies.

> *Waverley Steps* levels no tourist's eye on the boosted beauties of the 'grey metropolis of the North' but on a city washed by clean air, impregnated with Calvinism and its awkward by-products, owning tenements as well as castles. On a city whose civic conceit is backed by a cultural tradition and initiative that has contributed to the world something new and needed – the Festivals. To convey all this without a commentary by nuance and suggestion to one who, like myself, has never seen the City of Edinburgh is the signal achievement of *Waverley Steps* – a crisp, rhythmic film with brain and wit behind it.

> The camera picks out a few individuals, a few places; it follows a young Danish sailor to the drunken end of his day's shore leave and the newly married fireman of the 'Flying Scotsman' to his eager bed. Snippets of a bigamy trial, a lecture to medical students, a drayman placing a bet and winning, the long expected death of a tenement invalid, add up to a composite which needs no explanation or traditional British documentary lah-di-dah. And to which none is given beyond the overheard words and noises.

> The soundtrack is recorded on the spot by the simplest and most economic means, and cut into the action by a system of post synchronisation. Both visual and aural cutting are exemplary, sometimes masterly. This half-hour film

has, in fact, found something which should be pursued and developed.

I took a copy of *Waverley Steps* with me on a return visit to Stockholm and showed it to Sucksdorff. He sat silently. At the end he said that he could see clearly the influence of *Rhythm of a City*, but that *Waverley Steps* was much the better film.

5
Knowing Where to Go

Since *The Edge of the World* and *The Spy in Black*, Michael Powell had continued his film-making during the war, some of it, like *49th Parallel*, being in association with the Ministry of Information. He had formed an affection for Scotland, especially the Western seaboard, and knew that one day he would return. The opportunity came in 1944, while he was waiting for access to Technicolor to make *A Matter of Life and Death*.

Powell has told in his autobiography, *A Life in Movies*, how Emeric Pressburger said to him one day: 'I have always wanted to make a film about a girl who wants to get to an island. At the end of her journey she is so near that she can see the people clearly on the island, but a storm stops her from getting there, and by the time the storm has died down she no longer wants to go there, because her life has changed quite suddenly in the way girls' lives do'.

Powell asked: 'Why does she want to go to the island in the first place?' Pressburger replied: 'Let's make the film and find out'.

While Pressburger (in five days) was writing the story, Powell went off to look for the island. He found it eventually in Colonsay, between Jura and Mull, with the Corryvreckan whirlpool of fearsome reputation within reach to provide drama for the storm sequence. The unit made its headquarters at the House of Carsaig (Erraig in the film) on Mull and shooting went ahead in September. Wendy Hiller was the girl (she never reached the island), Roger Livesey was the impecunious MacNeil of Kiloran obliged to rent his castle to a rich Englishman, and Pamela Brown, 'half witch, half debutante', surrounded by a pack of Irish wolfhounds, was Catriona, descendant of the murdered girl who placed the Curse upon the MacNeils. There were parts for Finlay Currie and John Laurie (who, with help from Sir Hugh Roberton and the Glasgow

Orpheus Choir, made the ceilidh something to remember). Powell reveals in his autobiography that Livesey, appearing in a successful London West End play when the film was in production, never came within five hundred miles of Mull. A double was used on the island for the exteriors and storm sequence, edited with other material shot in the studio. The device, 'one of the cleverest things I ever did in movies' Powell thinks, did not seem to diminish the performances of Livesey and Wendy Hiller. The growth of affection between them was delicately done.

Powell sent a copy of the shooting script to me at the Scottish Office and asked for comments. Perhaps foolishly, I protested at the over-the-top scenes of the Irish wolfhounds gallumphing about Catriona's sitting room. Powell smiled and said, 'I knew you'd say that. I found just such a houseful of hounds on Mull'.

I Know Where I'm Going worked on me the charm it was to hold for audiences all over the world. This was not the stark reality of the deserted St Kilda but a gentle piece of imagined romance, touched by the strangeness of Hebridean myth and wildly dramatic when it needed to be, when the lovers are nearly drowned in the tidal race of Corryvreckan. The exteriors were shot in five weeks at the cost of one week's studio shooting. A fire engine from Fort William had to be hired to provide rain. So much for the nonsense about the hazards of making films in Scotland's weather.

When there was talk at this time about subjects for Scottish films, someone was certain to mention the story of Clyde shipbuilding. Who better to tell it than George Blake who had written so many novels in which the Clyde, river and estuary, played a part? Choice fell on *The Shipbuilders* (1944), adapted and directed by John Baxter who had shown in *Love on the Dole* and *The Common Touch* his understanding of the problems of everyday life.

Baxter both subtracted from and added to Blake's novel, while retaining at full stretch the Clydeside idiom. Opening in the depression of the early thirties, it traced the story of shipbuilding through the grim years of unemployment to the revival heralded by the decision to resume work on the Cunarder and the full tide of wartime work in the yards. The story was told through two characters, the

24. Shooting *I Know Where I'm Going*: Michael Powell (right) is explaining the routine to some local extras.

conscientious shipbuilder (Clive Brook) who could not believe that an island nation would allow shipbuilding to languish and who fought his battles mainly in the London shipping offices; and the honest, stubborn riveter (Morland Graham) who respected his craft and blindly put his faith in the ultimate re-opening of the yard.

There was what one critic called 'the solid truth of human experience' underlying the theme of Baxter's film. He did not attempt to provide a solution for the economic argument he so arrestingly presented, other than suggesting that war appeared to be the only route to prosperity for the industry. Shipbuilding was treated not simply as a background to a personal adventure but as an adventure in itself. The warmth of Glasgow life found expression even in the dereliction and gang-ridden streets and registered most strongly at a Hampden international. Nell Ballantyne gave a spirited portrait of the riveter's wife, and her performance added substantially to the film's human appeal.

As post-war film-making gathered momentum, producers began to look for subjects beyond the urban scene and the London West End stage. Among them was David Macdonald who, when in charge of the Army Film Unit, had directed such films as *Desert Victory, Left of the Line* and *Burma Victory*. He had read L. A. G. Strong's novel, *The Brothers*, when it was published in 1932 and had quietly nursed an ambition to film it. In 1946 he persuaded the novelist to give him the film rights. The producer was Sydney Box (of *The Seventh Veil*).

Uncompromising is the keyword for *The Brothers* (1947). This was no prettified tale set against a picturesque Highland background but a powerful story of love and hate among the crofters and fishermen of the West Coast. In the novel the location was Morar but Macdonald moved it across the Sound of Sleat to Skye, to its visual enrichment and without blunting the edge of its grim story of patriarchal family life: the time was the turn of the century. Always within the bounds of the theme he made full use of the spectacular setting of Loch Coruisk backed by the majestic Cuillins, written stiffly against the sky, and the tumbling cliffside village of Elgol.

At the centre of the story was a feud between two families, cherished with treachery and violence, which exploded with the arrival of an orphaned girl from a convent in Glasgow to be a servant in one of the families strong in its sense of moral rectitude. Two members of the family divide over her. What begins with murder ends with murder as the victim, with floats beneath his armpits and a herring tied to his cap, is dropped into the sea to become a fatally attractive target for a passing gannet with a bayonet-like beak to penetrate the man's skull. Justice is served, but no one is guilty.

The author drew on legend for this incident. And also for what was called the Rowing: a trial of strength by which a team from both feuding families, seated on opposite sides of the boat, determine which has the greater endurance by its ability to pull the boat off course. 'After the first mile . . . the men instinctively eased off. Already, as if by magic, they felt their animosity eased. That was the great quality of the Rowing; men who had striven against one another were almost always friends again afterwards'.

There was much colour of this kind to give character to the film. The Cursing, for example, in which seven stones are cast down by the head of each family, to the accompaniment of Biblically eloquent and corrosive invective; or the story of a woman who has turned into a seal, one of the oldest of Celtic legends.

Macdonald's use of his players added strength to the film. Their well-developed personalities were kept strictly under the director's control. Finlay Currie as the craggy head of one family had an unrelenting granite solidity. Duncan Macrae, whose acting skill was often squandered on trivial parts, gave a cutting edge of evil to the devious elder son, while Maxwell Reed was convincing as the marginally more likeable younger son. Will Fyffe made a jolly old rascal of the captain. Patricia Roc hardly fitted the accepted image of a Glasgow orphan but her low-cut chemise was enough to upset the jealous brothers. There was little warmth in the film. Its strength, undisputed, lay in the boldness of the theme and the courage of its treatment. Dilys Powell regarded it as 'another proof of the coming of age of the British cinema that we in this country are able to recreate so grim a poetic tragedy'.

25. Maxwell Reed and Patricia Roc in David Macdonald's *The Brothers* (1947): a powerful story of love and hate among the crofters and fishermen of the West Coast.

26. The wily islanders line up for *Whisky Galore!* (1948). Producer Monja
Danischewsky was amazed that film companies hadn't been fighting
over the rights of Sir Compton Mackenzie's novel ever since it was
published.

Close on the heels of *The Brothers* came another film from the North, *The Silver Darlings* (1947). This was an adaptation of Neil Gunn's epic novel of the herring fishermen of the Moray Firth. The novel had been welcomed by critics as 'a story instinctive with pride and undemonstrative passion, told with a power of physical evocation and a ripeness of human sympathy that together matter more than all else in story-telling'. There is no other Scottish novelist 'in whom the common touch quickens imagination so strongly – and none, it may also be, with a deeper feeling for the verities of Scots history'.

These qualities, alas, were not to survive translation to the screen. The film failed to strike a balance between its account of the fortunes of the herring fishing, improved when the government raised the herring bounty, and the study of the behaviour of a young mother who fears the sea because it has robbed her of her husband and now threatens to take her son away. There was some exciting photography of cliff scenery and storms at sea but there was no fusion of the fishermen's struggle to wrest a living from the sea and what was happening ashore. Back-projection for studio shooting still further reduced the impact of the film. The sequences of the press-gangs, in costumes out of *Iolanthe*, were hopelessly unconvincing and looked as if they might have been by another hand. Much better to have let the Scottish herring fishing story rest on Grierson's *Drifters*. Clarence Elder directed and also wrote the treatment. Muir Mathieson, who composed the music, must have been involved with the best of intentions and no doubt contributed to the suspense of the cliff-climbing sequences, the best part of a sad film which few had an opportunity of seeing.

A few years later there was talk of a film of Neil Gunn's *Morning Tide*. Robert Clark, head of production at Elstree for Associated British Picture Corporation, had the film rights and a shooting script had been written by Gilbert Gunn (no relation). The subject was raised with the producer over the next few years but the project went no further. Perhaps the subtleties of Gunn's writing could not be easily conveyed on the screen. None of his other novels were made into films. I thought *Bloodhunt* was the likeliest and sent my copy to several producers, unavailingly. It was later made into a successful film for television.

Of the films made on natural locations far away from the studios, much the most successful at this time was *Whisky Galore!* (1948). Monja Danischewsky, its producer, was restless at Ealing Studios. In 1947 he had been Sir Michael Balcon's publicity director for some ten years and wanted to do something more creative in film-making. He was told that if he could find a subject which could be made entirely outside the studios, he could produce it. He was familiar with Compton Mackenzie's novel and was astonished that film companies had not been fighting for the film rights since it had been published. It had languished untouched for a couple of years before Ealing bought the film rights. To Danischewsky, the wartime wreck of the S.S. *Politician* off the Isle of Eriskay and the salvaging by the islanders of its cargo of fifty thousand cases of whisky bound for the United States was a ready-made film story. It embodied a conflict, without which no film can succeed, between the crafty islanders, infinitely ingenious in obtaining and secreting the precious liquid, and the Customs and Excise men trying to suppress the illegal traffic.

Sir Compton insisted that the film be made on his home island of Barra in the Outer Hebrides. 'In no time at all', Danischewsky confessed later, 'I lost my heart to this enchanted island, and to the people who lived on it'. He chose as his director Alexander (Sandy) Mackendrick who was later to make many fine films in Britain and the United States but who at that time had no experience of directing. To Danischewsky Balcon protested, 'You don't know anything about production, dear boy, and now you are proposing to have a director who knows nothing about direction. I agree with you that Sandy should be given the chance to direct – but let him do it for the first time under a qualified producer. You go and get yourself a chap who'll make up for your own ignorance'. Mackendrick's enthusiasm for the project eventually prevailed.

Danischewsky took a unit of eighty with him to Barra. A church hall was fitted out as a studio and a smaller hall used as a projection theatre. They were on the island for fourteen weeks in the worst summer for years, with almost continuous gales. Danischewsky has described how tension developed between himself and Mackendrick who, with his Calvinist upbringing by a stern grandmother in Glasgow, disapproved of the islanders taking the whisky and found himself in sympathy with Captain Waggett, the Home Guard commander, waging war on the anarchist natives. The director's affection for Waggett (admirably played by Basil Radford) made him a more rounded character, an object of pity as well as a figure of fun. Danischewsky championed the cause of the islanders with equal determination. The result was a sharpened conflict and the film was all the better for it.

Mackendrick handled his players with a confidence surprising in a 'prentice work. Duncan Macrae demonstrated his comic skill as a befogged Home Guardsman, Gordon Jackson excelled as a timorous raw recruit dominated by his mother (Jean Cadell), Joan Greenwood gave a strange fascination to the postmaster's daughter and there were parts for James Robertson-Justice, A. E. Matthews and Compton Mackenzie himself as the captain. 'He made much of a small part but, on balance, I think he was right to stick to writing', was the producer's verdict. Father John Macmillan, a retired parish priest who lived in poverty in a small stone house overlooking the Atlantic and wrote poetry in ancient Greek, headed the cast of islanders whose performances blended well with the professional actors. An apt summing-up of the mood of the film was provided some years later by the daughter of the proprietor of the Castlebay Hotel, the unit's headquarters, who, when asked what it was really like having the film unit among them, replied, 'Och well, it was awfu' cheery'.

Whisky Galore! was an immediate success, whether it was shown under that title or as *Tight Little Island* in the United States and as *Whisky A-Gogo* in France and Italy. The gale of laughter it released took a long time to blow itself out in the faraway corners of the earth. It set a fashion in Scottish films – wily peasantry against interfering bureaucracy. It also did no harm to the Scotch whisky industry. The initial budget was £50,000, later increased to £85,000. The final cost ('thanks to the filthy weather that plagued us' – Danischewsky) was £107,000. Danischewsky was paid the same salary he had received

27. Gordon Jackson, James Robertson Justice and Joan Greenwood in *Whisky Galore!*: Jackson excelled as a timorous raw recruit and Greenwood gave a strange fascination to the postman's daughter.

as a publicity man – £80 a week – while Mackendrick was paid £35 a week.

Whisky Galore! was received with general critical enthusiasm. A comment made by William Whitebait (the always perceptive G. W. Stonier of *The New Statesman*) is particularly relevant to the subject of this book. 'I doubt if you will find Todday on the map', he wrote. 'The name is part of a prolonged chuckle over the idea of a Scottish isle going dry; but the place is real enough, and quite half the pleasure of *Whisky Galore!* resides in its unobtrusive sight-seeing. Atlantic rollers, the quayside where the steamer calls once or twice a month, the single flinty street, the prim kirk above, hills, sheep and clouds behind; authenticity of this kind brings its own reward. The makers of *Whisky Galore!* have planted themselves on the spot; and once there, they haven't succumbed to the holy awe or the unholy melodrama that usually overtakes such journeys. No unappeasable seducer is pecked to death by seagulls, and no clansman goes on playing the pipes till the waters close over his head. All is life-size and neat and humorously normal on Todday; or would be if, by the rigours of war, the islanders hadn't been calamitously cut off from their supply of whisky'.

Perhaps *Whisky Galore!* suggested a way forward. Perhaps small-scale films on Scottish subjects might have been the answer. Certainly they would have been nearer the everyday life of Scotland than some of the epics then in production or contemplation.

For years the life of Prince Charles Edward Stuart had dangled before producers like an overripe pear. If there had to be a historical theme here surely was the perfect combination – a handsome young hero, a brave adventure victorious nearly all the way, the loyalty of the Highlanders after defeat, a touch of romance. The sad ending in degeneracy in faraway Rome did not need to be included. To one film actor, Leslie Howard, Bonnie Prince Charlie was the very embodiment of youthful idealism. He said to me once at Denham: 'I have always felt that the story of Charles Edward, with its lesson of unquestioning loyalty to an ideal, should be the real expression of an undying Scottish national spirit'.

Knowing Where to Go

At Alexander Korda's London Film Productions Howard had in fact been cast for the part before his death in an air accident during the war. Korda thought of the subject as a Scottish national film to compare with *The Private Life of Henry VIII*. Michael Powell was among those who made an experimental approach. In his autobiography he writes: 'There is probably no finer story of two people on the run, helped by a few devoted friends to escape, but it had been so romanticised on highly coloured postcards and biscuit tins that, although I was so tempted, I feared it'. He describes how they planned and shot a sequence. Emeric Pressburger wrote it, Alfred Junge designed it, Jack Cardiff lit it, Hein Heckroth did the costumes, David Niven played the Prince, Pamela Brown played Flora Macdonald, Powell directed it. 'You would think there would be talent enough, but the piece was dead. The people in it never loved, never laughed, nor trod the heather'. They never made the film. It was to have been called *The White Cockade*.

But Korda was not so easily diverted. He believed in international films – big historical dramas like the Prince Charlie story or versions of famous novels like *Anna Karenina*. He committed his company, London Film Productions, to it. The treatment was written by Clemence Dane (why not Eric Linklater or Compton Mackenzie, both of whom had written, or were to write, books on Prince Charlie?). Probably producer rather than writer determined the style – everyone not only in the kilt but precisely in the right tartan for his clan, elaborate staging, much weighty dialogue, no humour.

At the root of the trouble was the selection of David Niven to play the Prince. In many films he had shown a light touch and a feeling for romantic comedy. Depth of characterisation was beyond him, try as he might. To make the Prince understandable on the screen there had to be development of character.

It always was a demanding role. Here was a young foreigner who arrived in Scotland, not with the troops the clan chiefs expected, but with only the Seven Men of Moidart. Yet when he raised his standard at Glenfinnan, chieftains and clansmen rallied round him although he was of a different world. There must have

28. *Bonnie Prince Charlie* (1947): joined *Mary of Scotland* as a monumental lost opportunity.

29. Finlay Currie and Irene Dunne in *The Mudlark* (1950): produced by 20th
Century-Fox at the time when American companies were obliged by law
to spend part of their profits in producing British films.

been charisma or magnetism of a high order to achieve this. Celebration at the Palace of Holyroodhouse and victory over Cope at Prestonpans were convincing enough and, as the Prince marched southwards on foot with his men, he had their respect. In one sense the confrontation with the clan chiefs at Derby when the Prince wanted to march on London was the most moving passage in the film, perhaps because there was an attempt to clarify the issues and perhaps because Culloden was casting its long shadow. The shambles of the battle was no more acceptable than it could ever have been. Thereafter the long trail through the heather, the caves, the pursuit and the loyalty of the Highlanders. The relationship between Charles and Margaret Leighton's ladylike Flora Macdonald was inevitably romanticised. There was no feeling of deprivation or hardship.

The film went into production in the summer of 1946. I saw some of the shooting in Lochaber and Glencoe. It was already clear that much money was going to be spent on even comparatively small details. The standard had been raised at Glenfinnan, with the monument carefully concealed from the cameras, and effort was being concentrated on making something exciting of the arrival of the clans. The route over the mountains by one group of eager clansmen was being filmed two thousand feet up on the northern slope of Buachaille Etive Mor in Glencoe where ten, twenty, forty kilted figures, claymores held aloft and plaids streaming behind them, were riding the scree to what, in the film, would be the meeting-place at the head of Loch Shiel. Why Glencoe? Because this was the most extensive and excitingly situated stretch of scree (and there were tons of bing refuse in reserve as a safeguard). The unit with its minders must have numbered over fifty. The cost must have been staggering. And all for, at most, thirty seconds of action on the screen.

In the studio shooting there was much the same attitude to detail. Michael Korda, son of the art director Korda brother, Vincent, described the making of the film in his book, *Charmed Lives*. At Denham Vincent expressed his approval of what appeared to be a Scottish moor in the Highlands but asked for more 'fissles' – and had to make a sketch of a thistle on the back of an envelope before his point was understood. The extras in the kilt filled him with dismay. 'All this orange and green – it's awful. On film it will look like a tin of marmalade'.

It was explained that the kilts had to be in the tartan of those clans which had supported Bonnie Prince Charlie, no matter how much he disliked the colours.

Michael Korda's verdict on the film, 'an expensive flop' is interesting, given his American viewpoint.

The appeal of Bonnie Prince Charlie as a movie story is fairly obvious, a romantic historical subject if ever there was one, but someone more familiar with American audiences than Alex might have questioned the box-office appeal of the Stuart uprising. Had it been based on a best-selling novel (and had it starred someone more popular in America than Niven) it might have worked, but instead it was a semifictionalised retelling of an event of very little emotional significance except to the Scots themselves, who were bound to be bloody-minded and nit-picking about any movie based on the life of their hero.

Only partially true as there were impartial verdicts on the film; but nevertheless *Bonnie Prince Charlie* joined *Mary of Scotland* as a monumental lost opportunity.

Two other less ambitious films with a touch of history should be on record. David Lean had made *Great Expectations* and *Oliver Twist* and was perhaps looking for another period subject. His choice fell on the story of Madeleine Smith, the young woman in Victorian Glasgow who was tried in 1857 on a charge of poisoning her French lover. The verdict was 'not proven', well known in Scots law but not elsewhere. Like others who have dramatised the affair, Lean had to walk a tightrope in his interpretation of the subject, here a script written by Stanley Hayes and Nicholas Phipps. Any deviation would have made clear innocence or guilt and had to be avoided. He was not helped by the performance in the leading part of Ann Todd (then his wife) who maintained her austere control even in what could have been scenes of passionate abandon to the blackmailing Frenchman (Ivan Desney). Other players included

Leslie Banks, Norman Wooland, André Morell, the Scots actresses Elizabeth Sellars and Jean Cadell, and Ivor Bernard as the chemist who sold Madeleine arsenic. Care had been taken with the sets (by John Bryan) reproducing Victorian Glasgow and the law courts in Edinburgh. I recall seeing Compton Mackenzie with Charles Bennett, Paul Sheriff and Carmen Dillon on a pre-production tour of Parliament Square and the adjoining law court where the trial took place. Although handled with sincerity and meticulous respect for detail, *Madeleine* (1950) could not compare in impact with Lean's Dickens films or with *The Bridge on the River Kwai* he was to direct a few years later.

The Mudlark (1950) was adapted by Nunnally Johnson from a novel by Theodore Bonnet about a Thames-side waif who sets his heart on seeing Queen Victoria, then wrapped in the deepest gloom in Windsor Castle, with no thoughts for anyone but Albert. His efforts to gain entrance to the Castle formed one element in the theme. The other concerned the relations between Disraeli and Victoria, the one anxious that she should end her long seclusion as the Widow of Windsor and the other determined to spend the rest of her days in the Castle, with Albert's memory to sustain her. A substantial influence on the outcome was John Brown's Scots commonsense. This provided Finlay Currie with one of his finest parts. The bluff Scots accents fell happily on northern ears and the mature balance of his performance helped to ensure that the film's sentiment never became sickly. Irene Dunne was a controversial choice for Victoria but she gave the Queen the required dignity and dumpy obstinacy. Alec Guinness was masterly as Disraeli, a performance which reached its climax in an eight-minute address to the House of Commons.

Directed by Jean Negulesco and selected for the 1950 Royal Film Performance, *The Mudlark* was produced by 20th Century-Fox during the period when American companies were obliged by law to spend part of their profits on the making of films in Britain. It was one of the better products of a temporary arrangement which helped to give continuity to British cinema.

Prod 65

30. Richard Todd in *Flesh and Blood* (1951): an adaptation of James Bridie's *The Sleeping Clergyman*, it continued the Scottish playwright's unrewarding association with the cinema.

6
Adapted from the Novel

A few years were to pass before the next spasm of costly film-making (*Bonnie Prince Charlie* was said to have cost a million). Other producers had taken note of the success of Ealing Studios, under the masterly control of Sir Michael Balcon, imaginatively producing for modest amounts films which were to the liking of audiences in Britain, with enough overseas distribution to make them worthwhile. Not all producers had his skill and judgment.

Floodtide (1949) was a minor British film, adapted from a novel by George Blake who collaborated with the director, Frederick Wilson, in writing the scenario. A conflict between rural and urban life was epitomised by the character of a farmer's son who gets a job in the shipyards where by dint of personal effort and hard study he becomes the firm's leading designer. The shipbuilding story reaches its climax when he saves from damage during a storm the ship he has successfully designed, while the personal story involves his romance with the boss's daughter. Sequences filmed in the studio did not always knit well with the shipbuilding scenes on the Clyde but the sense of being in Scotland was strengthened by the performances of Jimmy Logan, Elizabeth Sellars, John Laurie and Archie Duncan. 'The first recognisable portraits of Scottish working folk that we have seen on the screen', was the opinion of one contemporary critic. Gordon Jackson and Rona Anderson made the most of their parts: the starry-eyed idealist who marries the boss's daughter and the prim, correct, well-spoken young woman.

There was much that was recognisable, although not necessarily heart-warming, about the portrait of a Scottish soldier given in *The Hasty Heart* (1949), a straightforward adaptation of the stage play whose action hardly moves from a ward in a Burmese Hospital just after the war. The soldier, suffering from an incurable disease but unaware that he has only a few weeks to live, was played by Richard Todd, who tackled the part with the dour determination it demanded. Behind him lies a life of poverty and misery which to him justifies the isolation he feels from human friendship. Unlike him his fellow soldiers, including Ronald Reagan's American, know he is going to die and offer him their friendship for the last few weeks of his life; but, given his background, he is suspicious of kindness and relents only with the birthday gift of the full regalia of a Cameron Highlander. This was to be Richard Todd's strongest film performance. Although in a faraway setting it said something valid about the character of the Scot.

Another stage play to re-emerge as a film was *The Gorbals Story* (1950). In its original form Robert McLeish's dramatised account of the tribulations of Scottish slum-dwellers, as portrayed by the Unity Theatre players, had a pungent verisimilitude. In its transference to the screen, the play, in the opinion of a contemporary critic, had been 'both bowdlerised and vulgarised, its truth obscured and its pungency cheapened'. Gone was the richness of the Glasgow vocabulary, presumably in the hope of extending the appeal of the film, and as a result it lost a genuine sense of place. The film appeared to have been shot in semi-darkness, with the addition of a fog to intensify the obscurity. Something needed to be said at the time about social conditions in the Gorbals and a film with the realistic punch of *Housing Problems* might have achieved this, especially if it had retained the spirited sense of humour which is part of the character of Glasgow. It was a lost opportunity. *The Gorbals Story* remains a curiosity, interesting as a record, however imperfect, of an attempt to dramatise social issues and for the glimpses it gives of players like Roddy Macmillan, Archie Duncan, Andrew Keir and Russell Hunter. They were to appear to greater effect in other Scottish films.

James Bridie's unrewarding association with the cinema continued. *The Sleeping Clergyman* had been one of his most successful plays. When it was made into a film it was retitled *Flesh and Blood* (1951). Alterations were not limited to the title. Bridie's basic theme was that selective breeding in the human animal isn't necessarily a good idea. The setting was Glasgow and the story embraced three

31. Eric Woodburn, Fulton Mackay, John Gregson: an accident down the pit in *The Brave Don't Cry* (1952). Reviewing it, Dilys Powell wrote: 'Their reactions are the reactions of brave and ordinary men, hopeful, sardonic, showing a natural inclination to suspect that the best is not being done for them'.

32. Alex Mackenzie, Abe Barker and Jimmy Copeland in Alexander
Mackendrick's *The Maggie* (1954): Mackendrick needed no pressure
to recognise that the 'puffers' made ideal subjects for the film camera.

generations: a research student who dies of consumption before he can prove his genius, his daughter who is both a minx and a murderess, and her son, a bacteriologist who fights an epidemic, transferred, in the film, to an unspecified Mediterranean country. The film lacked visual treatment, sense of flow and rhythm, tension developed and sustained. Richard Todd had the central part, memorably created on the stage by Robert Donat, in the first and third episodes. André Morell's solidly persuasive performance as the sympathetic doctor who nurses the genius he detects was the backbone of the film. There were parts for Joan Greenwood as the provocative figure of the second generation and for Glynis Johns, who gave the final phase a warmth of appeal missing elsewhere. What had been something of a triumph for Bridie on the stage made an unsatisfying film. An incidental virtue may have been the reminder it offered of medical achievement at Glasgow University.

Flesh and Blood was followed by another adaptation of a Bridie play. At the end of 1950 John Grierson accepted the position of executive producer for Group 3, one of the co-operative film production exercises receiving loans of government money through the National Film Finance Corporation. John Baxter was appointed production controller. The chairman was Sir Michael Balcon. In June, 1951, it was announced that Group 3 would make five films, using first Southall Studios and later Beaconsfield Studios, evacuated by the Crown Film Unit after the government had decided to end official documentary film production. Studios meant that the new company had a working base. It also meant expensive overheads. Films had to be in production as quickly as possible, inevitably without adequate preparation.

So it was that Grierson, looking around for an easily produced film, remembered a play of Bridie's, *What Say They?*, which had the right mood – quizzical humour in everyday situations – which was characteristic of much of Group 3's production. The setting was Glasgow University and much of the film was shot on location at Gilmorehill. The director was Terence Egan Bishop whose earlier experience had been in documentary. If he did not show much confidence in handling the subject he was in good company as the diverse elements, including the biblical story of Esther, a subversive Irish poet working as the university gate-keeper, and student effervescence at Rectorial elections, had always been difficult to fuse satisfactorily. When the play was first presented at the Malvern Festival, the theatre critic of the *Glasgow Herald* wrote of 'this lax, random and languid fantasy . . . not even the expected amount of pawky humour, and anything like a binding moral or message, original or unoriginal, equally hard to seek'.

The players included Duncan Macrae, Charles Hawtrey, Patrick Barr, Joseph Tomelty and Robert Urquhart and there was a very small part, his first, for Ronnie Corbett. Production problems included the discovery, after the film was shot, that the plummy accent of one of the actresses did not carry conviction in the Glasgow setting. Molly Weir re-recorded the dialogue. When *You're Only Young Twice* (1952) emerged in London its treatment by the critics was at least as rough as the reception of the play had been. On the defensive, Grierson persuaded Walter Elliot, his and Bridie's friend, to write to *The Times* in protest, claiming that the film was 'fundamentally about the funny side of the immense seriousness of youth'. That did not save it, although it may have gone some way towards explaining the mood and the anarchistic spirit of the whole.

But much more successful Scottish films were on the way from Group 3. Grierson's boyhood had been spent among the miners of the Stirlingshire coal field. He had always wanted to make a film on a mining subject. Now he had the opportunity. On record was the near disaster at the Knockshinnoch colliery in Ayrshire where a sudden subsidence trapped miners below ground. Their eventual rescue made an epic tale on the lines of Pabst's *Kameradschaft*.

As writers Grierson called on Montagu Slater, well-known for his socialist sympathies and with much work of merit to his credit, and the like-minded Scottish author Lindsay Galloway. The story they produced had a three-fold structure: bravery below ground, the determination and resource of the rescue teams, and the reaction of the mining community. At its base was the conflict between the threatened tragedy and the will to survive, epitomised in the entombed miners, with the surface action as a kind of Greek chorus. Philip Leacock, the director, showed a clinical judgment in establishing and sustaining the suspense. One moment in the film was typical of its imaginative treatment. The miners, sitting idly below ground, are prey to all sorts of fears. To relieve the tension one of them begins to sing the Burns song, 'Flow Gently, Sweet Afton', perhaps unaware that the swollen waters of the Afton occasioned the subsidence. When the shot was taken Grierson protested that the singing sounded like a church choir. He prescribed a few drams of whisky to roughen the throat. Now the singing sounded like men suppressing emotion.

The players were drawn in the main from the Glasgow Citizens' Theatre – Andrew Keir, Fulton Mackay, Archie Duncan, Jameson Clark, Meg Buchanan and Jean Anderson: 'the best gang I have ever worked with', said Grierson. They stood close to their story in a way which seldom happened in British films. As Grierson said, if they were not acting themselves they were acting their next door neighbours.

The Brave Don't Cry opened the 1952 Edinburgh Film Festival (not without resistance from Wardour Street, whose production chiefs perversely did not want the Group 3 experiment to succeed). The reception was triumphant. After the Edinburgh showing Dilys Powell wrote:

> *The Brave Don't Cry* has the rare merit of never playing unfairly on one's emotions. The trapped miners are heroic but not impossibly saintly, and we are spared the familiar scene in which one of the party breaks out in uncontrollable hysteria. Their reactions are the reactions of brave and ordinary men, hopeful, sardonic, showing a natural inclination to suspect that the best is not being done for them. The contrast between their plight and the world of free air is drawn but not over-emphasised, and we are made to see that the groups above ground, the waiting rescuers and the women keeping watch, are also for the moment held in a tragic trap.

When it was shown in the United States later in the year, Bosley Crowther in the *New York Times* praised it highly. 'The varying moods of the trapped miners, the stoicism of their loved ones above ground, the creeping surrender to frustration and the final lift of

33. Paul Douglas, hard-pressed American star of *The Maggie*, whose exasperation with the skipper (played by ex-headmaster Alex Mackenzie) eventually mellows into something like respect.

heroism in the rescue – these things are beautifully articulated in the imagery of the screen'. The film became one the most widely shown of all the products of Group 3. Its value to Scotland was that it broke entirely with traditional conceptions. It was as far away from the heather and the haggis image as could be imagined.

Laxdale Hall (1952) was originally written by Eric Linklater as a treatment for Balcon at Ealing Studios (later expanded and developed into a novel). Grierson accepted it with relish. He liked the idea of simple peasant folk in isolated communities resisting long distance bureaucratic interference, unsympathetic and insensitive. Here was an excellent example: car owners in a remote Hebridean village refusing to pay road fund licences until they had adequate roads. Much fun was extracted from the visit of a parliamentary delegation, with a hapless Scottish Office official in attendance, intent on persuading the natives to see the unwisdom of their ways. The prospect of moving to a new town in the industrial Lowlands, where they could see neither the hills nor the sea, is anathema. 'I would as soon be in Hell as live in a place like that'. Perhaps the complications over the open-air production of *Macbeth* and the involvement of poachers from Glasgow weighed rather heavily on the comedy; but it had some glorious moments of fun, especially in all that concerned Roddy Macmillan's lugubrious undertaker.

John Eldridge directed, having collaborated with Alfred Shaughnessy on the script. In addition to such stalwarts from the Citizens' Theatre as Fulton Mackay, Jameson Clark and Andrew Keir, he had Ronald Squire as the leader of the revolt, Kynaston Reeves as a long-nosed and tough-as-leather parson and Raymond Huntley and Sebastian Shaw as the bemused parliamentarians. It was shot in Applecross and the road over the hill from Kishorn, as I recall, fully justified the reputation it had in the film's story. *Laxdale Hall* was a joyous film. Ignored by the London critics it was an instant success in Scotland. It ran for months in Inverness and for years after its first release, whenever an exhibitor knew early in the week that he had a flop, he would throw out a lifeline for *Laxdale Hall*.

Adapted from the Novel

It was followed not long afterwards by another Hebridean comedy. With the world-wide success of *Whisky Galore!* as an incentive, Ealing Studios were looking for another Scottish subject. Neil Munro's tales of the 'puffers' were recommended to them from more than one source. Sandy Mackendrick needed no pressure to recognise that the puffers, those chunky little flat-bottomed boats that used to ply between the Clyde and the Western Isles with their cargoes of coal, unloaded into carts after the vessels had berthed at high tide in sandy bays, made ideal subjects for the film camera. How to find a story to provide continuity and conflict? Munro's stories were examined and laid aside, reluctantly and respectfully: they were perfect little literary cameos which should be left undisturbed in their own medium.

With some help from William Rose, the screen writer, Mackendrick found his theme in the predicament of a hustling American business man, controller of an international airline, who entrusts his cargo, urgently needed for his new home on a Hebridean island, to the skipper of what turns out to be the most decrepit Clyde puffer still afloat. The skipper, a lovable old rogue, sees in this fortuitous commission an opportunity of earning enough to have the old craft repaired. When he realises what shipment by puffer means, the American is determined to have his belongings taken off and transferred to a fast cargo steamer. Out of this conflict of wills comes a steady flow of lively and amusing incident. It begins in Glasgow and moves to Crinan where, the last remaining possibility of having his cargo loaded on to a faster vessel having disappeared with the craftily contrived collapse of the old pier, the American decides to sail with the puffer to see that there is no further avoidable delay.

I saw some of the sequences for *The Maggie* (1954) shot at Crinan and marvelled at the director's patience and perseverance. In addition to the normal hazards of weather and light in exterior shooting there was the problem of the tide. By the time setting up and rehearsal were completed, the puffer made fast to the about to be destroyed pier and the Highland cattle, necessary for the scene, shepherded into place, the tide would work its inexorable changes and shooting would need to be delayed for a

89

day. Even so the weather next day could be entirely different and not match what had gone before or was to follow. Nevertheless the Crinan Canal sequences, especially the involvement in a poaching expedition of the American's prim London representative in bowler, umbrella and City clothes, were the funniest in the film. It gained immensely from its natural setting. Bowmore and Port Askaig on Islay were easily identified. More strongly in the first two-thirds of the film than towards the end, Mackendrick kept the comic invention going.

He was fortunate in his cast. Locked in conflict were Paul Douglas's bluff American, whose exasperation gradually mellows into something like respect, and the stiff and stubborn skipper of Alexander Mackenzie. The Scot was a retired headmaster who had appeared in one or two documentaries but whose first solid part this was. He seemed to exude the traditional Scots dominie's unshakeable authority and iron discipline.

Abe Barker, Jimmy Copeland and Tommy Kearins comprised his crew. A delightfully precise piece of fooling was contributed by Hubert Gregg as the prim Englishman while Andrew Keir gave a well judged performance as a newspaper reporter.

Perhaps these comedies did not bring us much nearer the real Scotland, if by that is meant the urban industrial scene; but they were authentic and genuine in their treatment of Scottish life. And enjoyable. Not every film needed to be immersed in social significance to be justified and worthwhile. John Grierson saw Neil Munro's Para Handy stories as

> an Odyssey of the common man with all his prides and his humours, wandering through the little places and getting a terrific bash out of life wherever he goes. That hard-bitten crew knew every trick of survival. Where its appeal lies is that it is the epic of the non-metropolitan, and a reminder that life is life and the same life wherever it is, and that you don't have to go to London – no, not even Edinburgh – to get the excitement . . . the whole point about Para Handy is that its one great thesis is – not being big but maybe a lot of nonsense, and the price of the little people is in making a splendid affair of being little.

34. Director Phil Leacock on location for *The Kidnappers* (1953), with the young stars Jon Whitley (left) and Vincent Winter.

A Scottish film but not a film about Scotland? *The Kidnappers* (1953) was adapted from a short story, 'Scotch Settlement', by Neil Paterson, included in the collection called *And Delilah*. Set in Nova Scotia at the turn of the century, it was filmed in Glen Affric, Inverness-shire, after the author and the director, Philip Leacock, had spent a month together in Canada, visiting typical communities, talking to people and taking photographs of backgrounds. They did not begin filming until they had the feeling of the story in relation to its background which was never far away from the Nova Scotia landscape. The short story itself was amplified and altered out of all recognition: Neil Paterson's Hollywood experience as a script-writer had taught him the different needs of visual and written media.

The Kidnappers is a study of a child's instinctive longing to love, or to be loved. It concerns two small boys, aged eight and five, who arrive at Cape Breton to stay with their grandparents and their aunt and find themselves in the midst of warring elements beyond their understanding. Their grandfather is a stern, unyielding man (he has lost his son in the Boer War) who has been brought up in a hard school and has no time for the gentler emotions. Characteristically he refuses to allow the boys the dog they wish and he disapproves of the romance between his daughter and one of the Dutch settlers, doctor to the community. A climax in the clash of wills is reached when the boys, starved of an object on which to lavish their affection, discover a baby in the woods and conceal it while the settlers search the countryside. Out of the commotion created by this kidnapping comes a new harmony in the relations between their grandparents and the other members of the community, and a more sympathetic understanding of the reason for the boys' unhappiness.

Philip Leacock counterbalanced the sentiment with humour and handled the theme throughout with a simple sincerity which lent it distinction. The strength of the film lay in the performance of Duncan Macrae as the boys' grandfather. He succeeded in suggesting the kindness hiding somewhere in the make-up of the stern, God-fearing old man. (I recall the astonishment of the technicians in the studio when I told them that Macrae was best-known in Scotland at the time as a comic actor of genius.) Adrienne Corri, curbing her natural vivacity, hinted at smothered fire in the portrayal of the old man's daughter while Jean Anderson was exactly cast as the grandmother. A further facet of Leacock's skill as a director was the way he coaxed reactions from the malleable faces of the boys, Jon Whitley and Vincent Winter. Sergei Nolbandov and Leslie Parkyn were the producers.

The Kidnappers made good use of the Glen Affric setting, a reminder that the rich and varied beauty of the Scottish country-side could be an asset in films which were not merely animated picture-postcards. The film was shown at the Cannes Film Festival in 1954.

It may have seemed that a solution had been found to the problem of making films on comparatively small budgets which could find a sufficient audience. There were still film-makers who thought, as Korda had, about big spectacular subjects for world markets. Among them was Walt Disney, whose choice of a Scottish subject was *Rob Roy* (1953). It had, after all, been 'the first Scottish epic' as long ago as 1922. Like that early silent film, shot around Loch Lomond with a cast of two thousand, it owed nothing to Scott. The story, written by Lawrence Watkyn, the American who wrote *The Sword and the Stone* and *Robin Hood*, was based 'on the legendary adventures of the famous Scottish adventurer, Rob Roy MacGregor'. Legend – not history, not fact. So be it.

Here we have a struggle between the rebel Rob Roy, who believes that Scotland's battles must be fought with the sword, and Montrose who is prepared to sell Rob Roy and his clansmen to the English for the sake of personal gain. Between them stands Argyll who believes in an honourable peace – an amnesty for the Highlanders and an end to bloodshed. When Walpole threatened to send an army into the Highlands to bring back Rob Roy, Argyll offers to go alone. He is too late to prevent more bloodshed. In the end all are happy. Rob Roy is pardoned and calls George a Great King to which the monarch replies in his halting English: 'You are a Great Rogue'. The Scottish case is fairly put and both Argyll and Lady Glengyle deliver words which many Scots found stirring.

By its own, never very high, standards *Rob Roy* was a polished piece of film-making. The story was told in terms of action and there were few moments when the screen lacked movement. There had clearly been a working understanding between Alex Bryce, who directed the location scenes, and Carmen Dillon, the art director, so that the film moved smoothly from exterior to interior. Such scenes as Rob Roy's wedding were handsomely done (however improbable) and there was a sense of style about the closing sequence at Buckingham Palace. The film had the wit to end where it began, in the Highlands, with Rob Roy exaggerating his victory over German Geordie. Harold French directed the studio sequences. Cedric Thorpe Davie composed the music for the film, including the mouth-music for the wedding dances.

Rob Roy enjoyed some more authoritative acting than was usual in films of this kind. James Robertson-Justice made a commanding figure of Argyll, and his scenes, with Michael Gough's self-centred and calculating Montrose, had an engaging edge. Jean Taylor-Smith made Lady Glengyle one of the pivotal characters in the story with a finely conceived performance. Richard Todd was a handsome and vigorous young hero without ever suggesting the kind of rogue Rob Roy must have been and Glynis Johns was a charming heroine. Barely discernible behind their bushy beards were Finlay Currie and Archie Duncan.

I saw some of the sequences for the film shot in the hills above Loch Ard in March, 1953. In place of the weather which might have been expected there was a drought! Day after day of clear skies and bright sunshine. Here men of the Argyll and Sutherland Highlanders, not long returned from Korea, fought out the battles between the opposing forces. The clashes between the Highlanders, with their targes and whirling claymores, and the redcoats backed by roaring cannon, were rich in the movement a film needs. Behind them the lightly misted hills, with snow-filled crevices here and there, provided the right background for some stirring action.

There was little of Stevenson left in *The Master of Ballantrae* (1953), another big, spectacular and expensive film, Scottish only in its scenic backgrounds. The story Stevenson wrote was jettisoned and in its place was a plot on routine lines about a feud between two brothers who both love the same woman. The older brother sides

35. Director Alexander Bryce and Forsyth Hardy (left) on location near Aberfoyle, for Walt Disney's *Rob Roy* (1953). By its own, never very high, standards, it was a polished piece of film-making.

with the Jacobites at the '45 Rising while the younger remains at home. After Culloden Ballantrae is forced to leave the country but before doing so is wounded in a duel with his brother, who thinks he has killed him. It was here that the film departed company with Stevenson. Overseas, Ballantrae joins company with a French buccaneer, amasses a fortune as a pirate and again returns to Durisdeer to find a dance in progress celebrating the engagement of his brother to the Lady Alison. Insults are hurled and rapiers are drawn; but when the redcoats dare to interfere in this family feud, the brothers sink their quarrels and are reconciled. By this time Stevenson was forgotten and the mood was strictly Hollywood.

Under some other title it would have been possible to accept *The Master of Ballantrae* as a lively piece of adventure, sustained at a spanking pace, and packed with exciting sword fights and hairsbreadth escapes. Errol Flynn made a dashing hero, Roger Livesey helped the swashbuckling mood with a cheerful performance as the Irish adventurer, and there was some convincing acting by Jacques Berthier as the French buccaneer. To admire without reservation was the photography of Jack Cardiff who caught the wild beauty of the Western seaboard and contrasted it with the sun-filled splendour of the Sicilian scene.

Film-making in Scotland was to reach its nadir in *Trouble in the Glen* (1954). This was an adaptation of Maurice Walsh's novel, produced and directed by Herbert Wilcox for Herbert Yates of Republic Studios in Hollywood. For the first few minutes it seemed that we were going to have an amusing film about Scotland. There was Orson Welles on the screen, his face aglow from the South American sun, saying what he thought about the country. After years of prosperous cattle-ranching on the pampas, he has returned to his ancestral home in the Highlands and does not like what he finds – the weather, the people, the roads, the fishing, the landscape. 'It's not a country', he explodes, 'it's the Dark Ages'. If only the film could have continued in this vein it would have been a delightful antidote to some of the too, too polite films about Scotland. But with the end of the lecturette wit faded out of the film and clumsy comedy and cloying sentimentality took over.

Again there was a kind of conflict between the expatriate laird who closes a road through his estate and the protesting villagers, thoroughly aroused. Among them is a little girl paralysed after a polio attack who finds the mirror outside her bedroom window sadly empty when the road is closed. To her rescue comes an American airman (she does not know he is really her father: she calls him Sir Lancelot) and he goes forth to do battle with the laird. On the way to the castle he meets the laird's daughter who, in playful mood, steals his trousers while he is swimming in the loch, so that he appears before her father, and a visiting bishop, in his shirt-tails. It was that kind of film. There were other complications with Highland cattle, released by the protesting farm-workers, roaming all over the glen and a threatened battle between tinkers and Glasgow toughs (which did not materialise). All ended happily, with the little girl looking forward to dancing down the re-opened road in the pink ballet shoes her father has given her.

A sad, bad muddle of unreal situation, forced humour and calculated sentimentality. There was not a genuinely fresh or natural moment in the film. Of the players only Orson Welles seemed to have an inkling of what he was doing, and seemed unperturbed by his final, monstrous appearance in the kilt. Victor McLaglen brought a bewildered bravura to his part as King of the Tinkers: it might not mean much but, begad, it was going to register. In tammy and tartan skirt Margaret Lockwood looked a little self-conscious while Forrest Tucker as the American seemed thoroughly embarrassed by the whole sticky business. The Scots, Moultrie Kelsall and Archie Duncan, could make little impact on the film. The scenery, normally a saving grace, was a muddy mixture of green and brown, aptly described by one critic as 'decayed sponge'. John Grierson, who said he had never laughed so much in his life, added that his one regret was that Laurel and Hardy weren't in the film. If they had been rounding up the cattle instead of Margaret Lockwood . . . Life in the glens was never like this.

At the end of this post-war decade came *Geordie* (1955), an adaptation by Frank Launder and Sidney Gilliat of David Walker's novel: a modest, diverting comedy which found its humour in comparatively simple ideas, developed in a heart-warming way. A gamekeeper's son, worried by his weeness, takes a correspondence course in physical culture and grows into a great, hulking giant. Prompted by his minister and encouraged by the laird, he takes up the sport of hammer throwing. Persuaded to enter for the local games he performs badly until the sight of his sweetheart appearing over the hill makes him throw the hammer almost out of the ground. Two members of the board for the Olympic Games are so impressed that they invite him to join the team for Melbourne. He agrees, on condition that he can perform in his father's Black Watch kilt. In the arena he fails until the visionary appearance of his sweetheart and the imagined sound of her voice bring about a transformation. A Danish blonde athlete marks his victory with a spectacular embrace, described in a broadcast commentary on the Games heard in his native village. Is reconciliation possible?

Frank Launder was greatly helped by his cast. Bill Travers had the physique for the grown-up Geordie and was also able to convey the obstinacy and single-mindedness of the character in a way which was likeable and not at all demeaning. Alastair Sim made an endearing fuss-pot of the laird. In one of his rare film appearances Jack Radcliffe made the minister one of the film's most convincing characters. The restrained naturalism of the domestic scenes with Jameson Clark and Molly Urquhart helped to set the mood of the film. Norah Gorsen's heroine was the film's one piece of mis-casting, unfortunate as the character was a major motivation in the theme.

Although it was shot in one of the worst summers (1954) on record, there was nothing to suggest the persistence of the lowering clouds over Aberfoyle, the main location. The Highland scenery greatly enriched the film. Someone had an eye for the Perthshire scene and brought it faithfully to the screen.

Geordie was a simple film. Its story could in a sense have been placed anywhere, from Poland to Peru. Launder and Gilliat were not trying to say anything significant about Scotland. They were attracted by the fantasy and fun in the original and saw how a comic situation could be satisfyingly sustained. There were the usual mutterings about misrepresentation when the film appeared. If Scots cannot take a joke they become themselves a joke.

36. Errol Flynn as James Durie (left) in *The Master of Ballantrae* (1953): Stevenson's story was jettisoned and in its place was a plot on routine lines about two brothers in love with the same woman.

Scotland in Film

Scottish films were still not being made by Scotsmen in Scotland. For good or ill they reflected the impact Scotland had made on the wider world. It was hardly surprising that the film-makers in Hollywood and elsewhere had seized, when making Scottish films, on the most easily identifiable elements in dress, character and background. These were, in the short term, assets in a visual medium. Scotland's experience was not unique. Think of any country in the world and how much the cinema has contributed, accurately or not, to the national image. If Scots wanted to change the image, or even influence it, they had to do it themselves.

7
Scottish Office Moves Half Way

When any form of government-financed film-making ended in 1952, Scotland lost the meagre flow of films which in any sense could be held to project the life of the country. There were large industries and corporations in the south which continued to make films in the documentary tradition established by Grierson (Shell, I.C.I., British Transport, Coal) but these were in the main about British or international subjects (British Transport under Edgar Anstey was an exception). In the years before the oil revolution they seldom reflected any activity in Scotland. This lack was noted at the Scottish Office, from which centrally financed film-making had been withdrawn as it had been from other departments of government. It was noted with concern. What could be done about it?

On file was the successful record of the pre-war Films of Scotland Committee. Why not revive this body? And so the wheels began to turn, slowly and ponderously as is the civil service way. The first organisation had been attached to the Scottish Development Council. Should the new one be a Committee of the Scottish Council (Development and Industry), similarly an independent body, encouraged but not directly financed by the government? If it were set up where was the finance to come from? The wheels turned ever more slowly; but the urge to use the film to project Scottish life and achievement was still there. At the Scottish Office there were public-spirited civil servants, notably William M. Ballantine, Director of the Scottish Information Office, who wanted it to happen.

And so the second Films of Scotland Committee was appointed in January, 1954. Its chairman was Sir Alexander B. King, the leading Scottish independent cinema exhibitor, and its honorary treasurer was Hugh Fraser (later Sir Hugh and still later Lord Fraser of

37. Orson Welles and Margaret McCourt in *Trouble in the Glen* (1954), the nadir of film-making in Scotland, apart from Welles's amusing lecturette.

38. Bill Travers, Brian Reece and Jack Radcliffe in *Geordie* (1955), a simple film which could in a sense have been placed anywhere, from Poland to Peru – and none the worse for that.

Allander). The members were representative of industry, tourism and local and national administration. They included John Grierson, whose experience of film-making now included the National Film Board of Canada, the Central Office of Information in Britain and the Group 3 experiment in story films, and Neil Paterson, author and screen-writer, who was in 1955 to win an Oscar for his screenplay adapted from *Room at the Top*. The remit given to the Committee by the Secretary of State was 'to promote, stimulate and encourage the production of Scottish films of national interest'. Its main resource, its only resource, was the enthusiasm of the members – 'the happiest and most selfless body I have encountered since I was in Canada', said Grierson.

When the formation of the Committee was announced by the Earl of Home, then Minister of State at the Scottish Office, Hugh Fraser made a gift of £10,000. In 1954 it was a larger sum than it will appear today. At most it might have made two or three modest short films. The theory was that industries, local authorities and national organisations would be persuaded to finance films which would serve their sponsor's purpose, be broad enough in scope to embrace the national theme and entertaining enough in treatment to be given distribution in the cinemas. Costs of administration and everything else were to be met from film exhibition revenues.

At the official luncheon to mark the inception of the Committee, Dr Christopher Macrae, then chief executive of the Scottish Council (Development and Industry), was overheard to say 'I give it a couple of years'. It was probably a generous time-scale. How could an organisation exist, far less prosper, in the expensive world of film-making on the flimsy and highly uncertain basis of income from short films made to sell goods or promote enterprise or otherwise serve a purpose unrelated to the entertainment of paying audiences in public cinemas? The formation of Films of Scotland had not been long completed before an inquiry came from the Welsh Office: 'Do you receive your government grant quarterly or annually?' There was silence when the inquirer was told there was no government grant.

Nevertheless twenty years and 150 films later . . .

Scottish Office Moves Half Way

In February 1955, I agreed to accept the appointment of Director of the new body and withdrew from the Scottish Office. It was not secondment in the civil service sense and there was no continuing financial obligation or remuneration of any kind, although Sir Charles Cunningham, in wishing me well, said that I was at the end of a string and could be pulled back. Why did I take on so onerous a task?

I had no illusions about the difficulties. I knew there would be a lot of hard work and little reward. The old cliché about meeting a challenge did, of course, apply. Possibly my range of experience over some twenty-five years persuaded me that I was as well equipped as anyone else at the time to tackle the job: ten years as film critic of *The Scotsman*, fifteen in charge of film-making for Scottish government departments, a founder of the Edinburgh Film Guild and the Edinburgh International Film Festival, friendship with John Grierson since *Drifters* and eventually his biographer, experience in public speaking, possibly a dogged determination to see an idea through to realisation, even an impossible idea.

Looking back I realise that it may have been a wrong course of action. If the Scottish Office wanted films made in the national interest it ought to have found money to pay for them. The longer I succeeded in making them the less was the likelihood of this happening. It has still not happened. While every other developed country – and many an underdeveloped one – has central finance for film-making, Britain has none; and any possibility of Scotland having any from a Scottish Assembly or any other form of independent administration disappeared with defeat at the 1979 referendum. Since then almost everything about film financing, film making and film exhibition has changed but not that.

Some of this frustration was expressed by John Grierson when he gave the Celebrity Lecture at the 1968 Edinburgh Film Festival. He spoke about the 'hand-to-mouth, beggar bowl existence which should never have been imposed on an organisation under so dignified an auspices'. The trouble in Scotland, he continued, had not been to find the cinematic skills. 'The trouble has been the lack of financial support to keep the skills in Scotland . . . appointed to great things, the Films of Scotland Committee has been shamelessly

105

39. *Enchanted Isles* (1957), made for MacBrayne's, could hardly miss since its subject was the ferry service to the Hebrides. With films about Aberdeen and Edinburgh, this was one of the first made by Films of Scotland.

40. Later, *Glasgow 1980* (1971) concentrated on urban transformation which made parts of the city barely recognizable.

starved of support. The fact that, in spite of all, it has contrived to make some films of quality is only the greater reason for deploring the neglect'.

There was a moment when it seemed possible that the case for support, so strongly made by Grierson, was going to be accepted by the Scottish Office. At a luncheon preceding the annual 'Scotland on the Screen' performance in August 1968 Grierson (later to be presented with the Committee's Golden Thistle Award for outstanding achievement in the film medium) was sitting beside William Ross, then Secretary of State. Both spoke afterwards, Grierson arguing that Films of Scotland needed central finance if it were going to do an adequate job for Scotland without the limitations imposed by sponsorship. In his reply the Secretary of State made what Grierson (and other members of the Committee present) took to be a commitment to help. Later, in pursuit of this, Grierson was a member of a small group from the Committee who saw the Scottish Secretary at the House of Commons. He listened. But no money was forthcoming. Grierson wrote to him in blistering terms (the letter is kept in an asbestos envelope at St Andrew's House) but it made no difference. If the will had been there, the course of film-making in Scotland could have changed.

For reasons I never felt able to accept, Willie Ballantine was opposed to the idea of any government money being made directly available for film-making. He had not been present at the luncheon and had not heard the exchange between Grierson and the Secretary of State. As he was the civil servant most immediately concerned with the affairs of the Committee, his advice must have been crucial. His opinion was that the films made by the Committee should have a purpose. I don't think he appreciated the limitations this imposed and the reluctance of the creatively-minded film-makers to accept them.

There was, of course, indirect government financial involvement. It was assumed that the various development boards set up by the government would have their films made through Films of Scotland, which was to their advantage as they knew that production would be supervised, objective respected and distribution arranged. The Films Division of the Central Office of Information looked to the Committee for films on Scottish subjects to send overseas and although the sums paid for overseas rights were pitifully small, there was the considerable advantage that print, language version and distribution costs would be met. It was better than nothing and it certainly gave Scotland a wider exposure overseas than any other part of the United Kingdom.

Nothing was ever easy at Films of Scotland. It is always difficult to persuade a Scotsman or a Scottish body to part with money. Paradoxically, given the city's reputation, the first local authority to do so was Aberdeen Town Council. Perhaps the sun does not shine so continuously or the beach always be so crowded with sun-seekers as *The Silver City* (1957) suggested; but there was John R. Allan in the couthy commentary he wrote and spoke to give it character and a sure sense of place. The councillors were satisfied, the citizens were pleased and the film secured distribution on merit. Its aim was the fairly simple one of attracting tourists.

Two other tourist films were in the first group. *Festival in Edinburgh* (1955) summarised all too briefly the range of the annual arts festival in the capital. Alastair Sim spoke the commentary written by Robert Kemp and the film had a circuit release – the first time any Scottish film had enjoyed such exposure. Robert Clark of A.B.C., a member of the Committee, helped to secure that. It was also adopted, as were most of the films, by the Central Office of Information for showing overseas in a number of language versions.

Enchanted Isles (1957), made for MacBrayne's, could hardly miss since its subject was the ferry services to the Hebrides. It was finely photographed, especially the sequence on Staffa, and on the whole justified its title. The commentary was spoken by Fulton Mackay who knew the islands well and whose first link with film-making this was. It went straight into the cinemas. Sir William Robieson, editor of the *Glasgow Herald* and a director of MacBrayne's, had helped to have the commission placed with the Committee.

In time, there was a pattern of tourist films covering the whole country, from the Shetlands to the Mull of Galloway, from St Kilda (an outstanding film made by Christopher Mylne) to St Andrews (an equally impressive film by Mark Littlewood). Some, like *Perthshire*

41. Ron Geesin (left) and Billy Connolly in Murray Grigor's *Clydescope* (1974), a lively exception to run-of-the-mill tourist films.

42. *As Long as You're Young* (1962): celebrating the success of the Scottish Youth Hostel movement.

Panorama (1959), enjoyed such a wealth of visual beauty that it could scarcely be contained in twenty minutes. It was backed by Neil Paterson's commentary, as well informed and phrased as we would expect from an author living in the heart of the county. Others, like *Glasgow 1980* (1970), concentrated on urban transformation which made parts of the city barely recognisable. *The Quiet Country* (1972) explored the south-west, by-passed in so many tourist films of Scotland, while *Lothian Landscape* (1974) put revealingly on record the towns and villages of East Lothian and the serene tempo of life there.

Ayr, Rothesay, Greenock, Paisley, Inverness, North Berwick, Stirling, Dunfermline, Kirkcaldy, Lochaber, Skye, Iona, Rhum – they all had their films. So much patient negotiation summarised in a line or two!

Many of the tourist films followed conventional lines. A lively exception was Murray Grigor's *Clydescope* (1974) which brought Billy Connolly to the screen. This was an ingeniously assembled kaleidoscope of river and estuary, town and country, with Connolly as the man who came up the Clyde on a bike, impersonating in turn a Border minstrel, an Edwardian Rothesay pierrot and a Glasgow folksinger. He was also to be found with his banjo on the deck of the veteran paddle-steamer, the *Waverley*: the aerial shots of the vessel weaving among the islands of the Clyde estuary gave the film its most memorable moments. Another highly successful tourist film was *The Line to Skye* (1973) on the much threatened railway from Inverness to Kyle of Lochalsh. Here Eddie McConnell's always sensitive camera caught the beauty of a richly varied landscape while Muir Mathieson's music subtly emphasised the changing rhythms of the train as it sped towards the distant Cuillins. It had the good fortune to go round the cinemas with *The Sting*, which meant large audiences and long runs everywhere.

Supplementing these tourist films were others dealing with various cultural subjects. One of the earliest was *Scotland Dances* (1957) on Scottish country dancing, popular all over the world. Its appeal in Iceland could perhaps be understood but in Morocco? It was made for the Royal Scottish Country Dance Society and included

112

a sequence shot in Cape Town in the shadow of Table Mountain. *Songs of Scotland* (1963) imaginatively linked some familiar melodies, including 'Kishmuil's Galley', 'Loch Lomond' and 'John Anderson My Jo'. *As Long as You're Young* (1962) celebrated the success of the Youth Hostel movement with impressive photography of young people on the move through some of the most spectacular areas of the country including Glencoe. George Bruce's poetic commentary was spoken by Bryden Murdoch. Writer and narrator were to work together on several of the films, to their unquestionable enrichment. Tom Fleming was another narrator whose contribution went creatively beyond the delivery of a commentary. He was involved in the making of one of the films on the Edinburgh Festival, a tantalising subject in the sheer concentration of activity in all the arts. *Walkabout Edinburgh* (1970) had Eddie McConnell following Richard Demarco as he moved around the city, enthusing about the villages within the city's boundaries and losing his bonnet on the windy ramparts of Craigmillar Castle.

Painting and architecture provided subjects for several films, made in association with the Scottish Arts Council. *Three Scottish Painters* (1963), on John Maxwell, Joan Eardley and Sir Robin Philipson, was one of the earliest and its record of the artists at work, especially Joan Eardley who was to die not long after the completion of the film, was uniquely valuable. *Still Life with Honesty* (1970), on Sir William Gillies, directed by Bill Forsyth and with commentary spoken by the artist, captured the personality of a well loved painter and teacher. *Mackintosh* (1968), on Charles Rennie Mackintosh, was a labour of love for Murray Grigor, then Assistant Director at Films of Scotland. He was to follow it with an equally distinguished film on Robert Adam, *The Hand of Adam* (1975). The 200th anniversary of the New Town of Edinburgh was the subject of *Prospect for a City* (1967). David Bruce, then my assistant, made *The Sun Pictures* (1965) on the work of the pioneer photographer David Octavius Hill.

Scotland's writers presented rather more demanding subjects, without obvious visual elements. *The Practical Romantic – Sir Walter Scott* (1969) used Abbotsford and the Border country in its biographical approach. Documentary in style, it could not have the

113

43. *Seawards The Great Ships* (1961): most cameramen in Scotland shot material for the film, and every launching for a year was covered. The result became a classic of documentary film-making.

44. The Wallace Monument from Stirling Castle: John Grierson's personal film of his native Stirling: *The Heart of Scotland* (1962).

drama a personal film would have had, but it served its purpose. *Hugh MacDiarmid: No Fellow Travellers* (1972), written by Douglas Eadie, had the poet in one of his gentler and less pugnacious moods. *A Stone in the Heather: Eric Linklater 1899 – 1974* (1976) included interviews with the author in Orkney. Linklater also appeared – in kilts in an astonishing range of tartans – in *The Prince in the Heather* (not made for Films of Scotland) a bland account of the Prince's wandering in the Highlands and islands after Culloden. Douglas Eadie wrote and directed *Sorley Maclean's Island* (1974), much of it shot on Raasay and including the poet reading one of his poems in Gaelic. Another poet, Robert Garioch, read his poem, *Sisyphus* (1971), illustrated in cartoon form by Donald Holwill. *Light in the North – Neil Gunn* (1971) was a brave attempt at the impossible – to bring to the screen a gentle, reserved, always courteous man who would with great reluctance talk about his work and hardly ever about himself. 'A man survives through the influence he has had on others, who grow because of him', wrote his biographer. Perhaps the film helped the process of survival.

When I was appointed Director I made a list of a hundred films I would like to see made. One of the most ambitious, *Loch Lomond* (1967) was not the obvious tourist film but a study of what happened around the loch when the tourists had departed: the shepherd gathering in his ewes for the dipping, the game warden watching a salmon struggling into the loch after spawning in the upper waters, the research biologist taking samples from the water, the farmer, the publican, the postman delivering letters to the islands, and the travelling shop-keeper. To their stories was added the wildlife of the area, from the deer on the high tops to the water birds round the loch side. It was a film of lasting value, made with warmth and affection. Laurence Henson directed with Edward McConnell as cameraman. William McIlvanney wrote the commentary, spoken with feeling by Alec Clunes.

Included in my original list were films about Prince Charlie and Mary Stuart. I thought it might be possible to tell the story of the Prince entirely, or almost entirely, in terms of song. A romantic rather than a realistic image certainly, but that was how his life had been represented by the ballad-makers. There was no money for it but I was able to persuade Drambuie to finance it, given their interest in the origin of their liqueur. John Grant, my then assistant, did the research and wrote the treatment. *A Song for Prince Charlie* (1959) was directed by Hans Nieter O'Leary, the subject making a strong appeal to the Gaelic side of his nature. The film was one of the most popular made by Films of Scotland. It was criticised for its perpetuation of a myth. But praise came from an unexpected quarter, the normally difficult-to-please *Monthly Film Bulletin* of the British Film Institute: 'An unusually intelligent and distinguished little film. Not only is the Technicolor used with skill and restraint, but the commentary is most successfully integrated, while the ballads are a constant joy'. James Cameron wrote the linking commentary, narrated by Duncan McIntyre, and Walter Lassally photographed the Skye sequence.

The film on Mary Queen of Scots was never made. I wrote a treatment for a documentary which would tell the story against the background of the chateaux, palaces and castles in which she lived: her comparatively happy years in France – wedding at Notre Dame, honeymoon at Chenonceaux – contrasted with the turbulent years in Scotland at Holyroodhouse, Edinburgh Castle, Linlithgow Palace and Falkland. When I visited Dundrennan Abbey, where she spent her last night in Scotland, the crows were hovering over the tall trees which surround the ruined building. It would have been a fitting image, I thought, for her sorrowful departure.

All was not sweetness and light in the Scottish films I produced. At least a third of them were about industry, what Scotland made. That was after all an important part of the remit given to the Committee.

One of the first was a film about hydro-electric development, then spreading through the Highlands, urged on by Tom Johnston who had become chairman of the North of Scotland Hydro-Electric Board he had established while Secretary of State. The financing of the film involved approaches to about twenty of the firms constructing the dams and generating stations. One managing director of a London-based company strongly resisted my pleas and made some slighting reference to Scotland. My hackles rose

117

and, assuming that the case was lost, I spoke out loud and clear. Suddenly he opened the top drawer of his desk. I feared he was going to pull out a revolver. Instead he produced his chequebook and said 'How much do you want?' Grierson wrote and spoke the commentary for the film (the only occasion in his life he did so). Other films had been made on hydro-electric development and the obvious titles – *Power for the Highlands*, etc. – had been used. At 2 a.m. one morning my phone rang. Grierson was phoning me from Calne, his home in Wiltshire. 'I've got your title', he said, '*Scotland be Dammed'*. Cravenly we put it out as *Rivers at Work* (1958).

Another of the early industrial films was *From Glasgow Green to Bendigo* (1961). I can still recall Sir Alex King's astonishment when I told him we were going to make a film about carpets. 'Carpets!', he said 'Who will want to see a film about carpets?' The first attempt at a treatment was not promising. I explained that what I wanted was a film primarily about the designing of carpets, how the shapes were chosen and how the patterns evolved. The result was a fascinating film which, among other things, told how James Templeton and Company had supplied carpets for the White House, for parliament buildings all over the world and for the coronation of Queen Elizabeth at Westminster Abbey. Ambitiously it had a circuit release with *Spartacus*. The managing director of the company, registering at a Sydney hotel and entering his occupation as 'carpet manufacturer', was told by the receptionist that there was a film about carpet-making showing at a cinema along the street. It was *From Glasgow Green to Bendigo*.

There were films about all the major industrial developments of the period: the steel strip mill at Ravenscraig, the aluminium smelter at Invergordon, the experimental pumped-storage scheme at Cruachan, the building of the road bridges over the Forth, the Tay and the Clyde at Erskine, the completion of the road through the Highlands to Inverness, later the boring for oil in the North Sea. There were films on all the new towns – East Kilbride, Cumbernauld, Livingston, Irvine, Glenrothes. A new whisky distillery at Tormore and several very old ones elsewhere were celebrated. In the sixties there was growth all over the country. Promise and progress were in the air. It would have been strange indeed if this had not

45. The Barra coastline, from *A Pride of Islands* (1973): scripted by Allan
Campbell Maclean, photographed by Oscar Marzaroli and Martin
Singleton, shot mostly from the air.

been reflected in films made by a body given the responsibility of recording Scottish life and achievement.

One of the industrial films was to become a documentary classic. A film on Clyde shipbuilding had been high on the list of subjects I prepared. When I first approached the Clyde Shipbuilders' Assocation, with the help of Sir Eric Yarrow, a member of the Committee, there was little enthusiasm. Their order books were full, they said. A film would be an embarrassment. It was 1960 and the post-war boom in shipbuilding was still bringing customers to the Clyde yards. There were twenty-three of them on the Clyde river and estuary. On the understanding that none of the yards would be named on the screen or in the commentary, they eventually agreed to share the cost equally with the Central Office of Information, who wanted a film on the subject for showing overseas. John Grierson was persuaded to investigate and write a treatment (a penetrating piece of writing subsequently published in the 1968 Edinburgh Festival programme). He had seen and been much impressed by the work of a young American director, Hilary Harris, at the Brussels Experimental Film Festival in 1958. It seemed as if he might bring a fresh eye to bear on a much-filmed subject. After problems over a work permit had been overcome he was given the film to direct and spent a year familiarising himself with the products of the yards. He worked with Robert Riddell-Black of the Glasgow company, Templar Film Studios.

Most of the cameramen in Scotland shot material for the film, in addition to the director. Every launching for a year was covered. Harris had been told by Grierson that he must open the film with a spectacular shot which would immediately grip audiences. He arranged for a camera to be placed on a platform just above the propellor of a ship about to be launched, and wires were led to the deck so that he could operate it. It was a very hot day on the Clyde and the vessel entered the water with a force no one had been anticipating. Platform and camera sank out of sight. Harris was dismayed. 'Don't worry', the foreman told him, 'we could get a cigarette-lighter from the bed of the river'. A diver was sent down and the camera retrieved. The laboratories were consulted and he was told to extract the exposed film and send it to them. Success! And so the dramatic shot which opens the film was one which was rescued from the bed of the river.

Cliff Hanley wrote the commentary, spoken to maximum effect by Bryden Murdoch. *Seawards the Great Ships* (1961) won more international recognition than any other short film of its period, culminating in a Hollywood Oscar in 1961. It was a film about the craft of shipbuilding. It was never meant to be a film about the life of the shipyard workers, as some blinkered critics suggested it should have been. If that had been the intention, Grierson, founder of the social documentary school of film-making, would have written a very different treatment. It went round the Rank cinemas in good company, with *Tunes of Glory*.

A number of ambitious films were made for the Highlands and Islands Development Board, set up by William Ross when Secretary of State and with Sir Robert Grieve, later a member of the Committee, as its first chairman. *In Great Waters* (1974) was about fishing today – not *Drifters* any longer but science in the service of the industry, the herring located by sonar, a hundred tons caught in a giant purse-net and pumped aboard. Elsewhere the lobster-men were seen placing their pots at the foot of the Old Man of Hoy, an armada of boats were landing their catches at Mallaig and at Lerwick fish were being processed for the market. A story of great importance to Scotland was told with strength and conviction by Laurence Henson and the visual splendour of the subject was vividly caught in Eddie McConnell's photography. Why, I wonder, has so much of it gone from the memory while *Drifters* remains as clear as ever?

A Pride of Islands (1973) was photographed mainly from the air: the aeroplane was now the preferred way of reaching the Hebrides quickly and the aerial photography showed how dramatic the scene could be: the labyrinthine lochs of Barra, the pattern of the fields in varying shades of green in Orkney, the fringe of yellow sand and the deep blue of the sea, shimmering in summer light. In Stornoway the islanders put their skills into the weaving of Harris tweed, from Kirkwall the walking wealth of cattle-rearing Orkney, worth on export over two million pounds a year, in Lerwick, a town that looks to the sea and lives from the sea, the fishermen are joined by the oilmen, operating from off-shore islands of steel. Allan Campbell McLean's well informed script and commentary provided a firm basis for the film, given visual distinction by Oscar Marzaroli and Martin Singleton.

Highlands (1971) by the same group, with Bill Forsyth as editor, concentrated on change in the area – the aluminium smelter at Invergordon rather than the stag at bay, the power station at Cruachan rather than the shaggy Highland cattle at the water's edge in misted glens, the great forests on the slopes of Mam Ratigan feeding the pulp mill at Corpach rather than the golden eagle soaring above them. There were further contrasts in the sand yachting at Dunnet Bay, ski-ing at Aviemore and sun bathing round Loch Morlich. Not a kilt or a piper in sight.

Earlier, several more modest films had increased the range of coverage of an area which might have been designed for the camera. Murray Grigor's *Travelpass* (1973) was a light-hearted impression of the ease of travelling in the Highlands and islands as seen through the eyes of two London-based girls who travel by train, bus and boat, contrasted with the difficulties experienced by two young men in a red sports car who set out from London on a similar touring holiday.

Highland Crafts (1973) showed the increasing number of artists and craftsmen who live and work in the area, some of them in the craft village of Balnakiel, fifteen miles from Cape Wrath. *Islands of the West* (1972), directed by Bill Forsyth, concentrated on the beauty of the Hebridean scene, photographed from the air and on land and ending with the great stone cross at Callanish with its sense of a long-lost civilisation.

The H.I.D.B., as it is familiarly known, was one of the most understanding of the government financed bodies served by Films of Scotland. By the end of the association it had a range of films in which in conception and quality a sponsor could take pride.

Fashions in short films were changing. Television provided an outlet for documentaries which could reach a very large audience in the shortest possible time. Cinemagoers were no longer prepared

46. Orson Welles in his own *Macbeth* (1948): 'a detestable man until he became king, then once he is crowned, he is doomed; but once he is doomed, he becomes a great man'.

to look at films which did not have a story and which appeared to have a propaganda purpose, however well disguised. There was no longer a ready market for short films, and revenue from their distribution had declined.

It had been the practice at Films of Scotland for any surplus revenue to be used for making experimental films innocent of any other purpose. On one occasion Eddie McConnell was invited to make a film about the colour of Scotland, the treatment to be entirely of his choosing. The result was a delightful little film called *A Kind of Seeing* (1967). In colour certainly, and shot in Scotland, but otherwise impossible to categorise. He could make of the reeds on the shores of Loch Lomond patterns of beauty holding a subtle pleasure for the eye.

A more ambitious experimental film was *The Duna Bull* (1972) which marked Films of Scotland's entry into the world of the story film. It was based on an incident described to me on a visit I paid to the island of Foula, setting for Michael Powell's *Edge of the World*: the death of the island's only bull, on whose service to a small herd of cows the islanders depended for their calf subsidies and much else besides. After prolonged correspondence, achieved with difficulty, between the isolated islanders and the Department of Agriculture, the bull is dispatched from the mainland in a fishing boat which, in the height of a storm, sails round the harbourless island for three days. In the end the bull is pushed overboard and told to swim for it. It survives (unlike the experience of a bull at Vatersay in the Shetlands which made the headlines early in 1988). The story was developed by Cliff Hanley, with invaluable guidance from Neil Paterson. It was directed by Laurence Henson who had previous experience in handling actors and dialogue in *Flash the Sheep Dog* and *The Big Catch*, made for the Children's Film Foundation. Successful everywhere in the cinemas, the film won an award at the Melbourne Film Festival where it was described as 'one of the highlights. It could well be used as an object lesson on how to make a very good story about some of the problems which arise in isolated communities'.

A second story film, *The Great Mill Race* (1975), on the woollen industry of the Borders, was based on a true experience: a sheep

124

shorn in the morning, its fleece spun into thread and woven into cloth, and a suit made, all in a day. The idea was developed by Alasdair Gray (of *Lanark* fame) and a fast-moving film carried its improbabilities lightly. Robin Crichton directed with confidence.

Given time, this departure into story film-making might have grown into something more substantial. Ideas for films were emerging and there was ambition in plenty. This was the moment for the small miracle, in financial provision, which would release ambition and make it real.

When the Committee was set up, there were two or three small companies in Scotland making occasional industrial or educational films. Among them were Campbell Harper Films in Edinburgh, Thames and Clyde Films in Glasgow and Templar Film Studios. None had experience of making films which had gained general release in the cinemas. Since that was essential for the continuing existence of Films of Scotland, the first film commissions had to be placed with London-based companies, notable among them being the largely Scottish staffed Anglo-Scottish Pictures, successful producers of many of the early films. Alan Harper's company made several films including *The Good Servant* (1958), on the Clydesdale horse, *Prospect for a City* and films on the Forth and Tay road bridges. Stanley Russell of Thames and Clyde made *Playing Away* (1961). Robert Riddell-Black and his associate David Low produced a number of films, and their company was a training ground for others who formed their own units: Laurence Henson and Eddie McConnell formed IFA (Scotland), Charles Gormley and Bill Forsyth founded Tree Films, Oscar Marzaroli and Martin Singleton set up Ogam Films. Mark Littlewood and Mike Alexander, both trained by Alan Harper, became Pelicula Films. At Nine Mile Burn south of Edinburgh, Robin Crichton operated independently as Edinburgh Film Productions. Murray Grigor's company was called Viz Films. They all readily accepted the commissions that came from Films of Scotland while increasingly making it clear that they were ready to go it alone (as, of course, they could have done at any time). It was a healthy omen for the future of Scottish film-making.

125

47. Welles's *Macbeth*. Everything was darker or larger or bloodier or more violent than the original, of which very little of the text, ruthlessly mauled, remained.

48. Peter Sellers (left), directed by Charles Crichton (right) in Monja
Danischewsky's *The Battle of the Sexes* (1959): a young American
woman efficiency expert has a disturbing impact on an old-established
Edinburgh tweed-making firm.

In 1957 I proposed that the first group of six films should be shown at a special performance, 'Scotland on the Screen', during the Edinburgh Film Festival. Sir Alex King was sceptical, as one would expect a major cinema exhibitor to be. 'Are you showing them in the news theatre?' I said that what I had in mind was the Regal, with a seating capacity of 2,750. 'You're mad', said Sir Alex and went off on holiday to Nairn. A day or two before the performance he phoned and asked how booking was going. I told him there were about 50 seats unsold. 'I'm coming down', he said.

This was the beginning of a series of annual performances at the Festival and at the Royal Festival Hall in London. These were shop-windows for the Committee's films and helped to make its work known. In 1962 in response to the urging of Sir Hugh Fraser, I took a programme of the films on a tour across Canada, from Halifax to Victoria, and repeated it every second year, later including cities in the United States. In 1969 I toured Australia and New Zealand. Interest in the films was phenomenal. The huge Jubilee Auditoria in Edmonton and Calgary were full. In Vancouver the police could hardly control the crowds trying to gain admission. In Perth, Australia, the theatre could have been filled twice over. In Adelaide the largest cinema in the city was not large enough.

In the beginning it seemed as if émigré audiences wanted to see the Scotland they had left behind: the heather on the hill and the cottage by the loch side. Natural enough. In time, however, they saw that Scotland was changing and that the here and now was not like the yesterday they had known. There was applause certainly for *A Song for Prince Charlie* when it was shown; but a few years later the same audience was applauding *The Hollow Mountain* (1966) – the construction of a power station in the heart of Ben Cruachan. At a performance at St Petersburg in Florida a Scot was furious because the programme did not include the Oscar-winning *Seawards the Great Ships*. In Australia there was a delighted response to the introductory sequence of *Weave Me a Rainbow* showing the birth of a lamb, as if an urban audience were seeing it for the first time. At the Sydney performance the son of the Loch Lomond boat postman was in the audience. Such anecdotes could be continued *ad infinitum*. The performances must have done something to correct the heather and haggis image. They also earned revenue, as did all the performances in Britain and overseas.

At the end of twenty years, therefore, the sheer volume of film-making about Scotland was prodigious. Most of the films would not have been made but for the focus created by the Committee. The toil and the trouble had been worthwhile and 150 films were there to prove it. On my retirement the Committee, now with George Singleton as chairman and Andrew Stewart as vice-chairman, entertained me handsomely to dinner, with all those who had been associated with us; and the film-makers themselves invited me to dine with them in Edinburgh, a gesture I took as gratitude and one I shall not forget.

I retired for a number of reasons, not all relevant to the subject of this book. In a sense Films of Scotland was an idea whose time had come – and gone. Television had made a fundamental change in the situation, providing an outlet for the kind of short films we had been producing but without yielding the kind of revenue cinema showing had made possible in the earlier years of the Committee's existence. The individual companies, now numbering a dozen or so compared with the sparse film-making capacity in 1955, could produce films directly for television without the involvement of centralising direction. In twenty years I had raised £750,000 to finance the production of 150 films. The flow of commissions, none ever declined by any of the companies, must have helped to provide an economic basis for their activities, assuming there was other work – as there certainly was – obtainable on their own initiative. Now they could look to television, or to feature film-making, without concern for national projection.

Perhaps an impartial Englishman should have the last word. John Chittock, writing about a proposal to set up a similar body in Ireland (*Financial Times*, 6 January, 1976), said:

This idea takes as its model the Films of Scotland Committee, which since its formation in 1954 has been responsible for about 150 films. This Scottish committee has acted as a promotional and pressure group, educating industry to make greater use of film, but primarily as a national rather than commercial instrument. Its success has been without equal in the

129

world and no doubt Scottish national feeling has been fortified by many of the glorious films the committee has inspired.

The Committee was faced with an increasingly difficult situation: a decline in the revenue from the distribution of short films, the resistance of audiences and cinema managements to any film with a promotional purpose, the eagerness of the Scottish film companies to make films, including feature-length fiction films, independently and the fact that television had materially altered the opportunities for film production and exposure. There was still no direct Government aid. The Scottish Film Production Trust, established with monies I had obtained from the always supportive Scottish banks, helped with the financing of one or two films, including one on Iona, *Dove Across the Water* (1981), partially funded by the Hugh Fraser Foundation. There was a film, *Highland Highway* (1981), co-operatively financed by the contractors on the A9, the highest trunk road in Britain, and a charming short film, *The Grand Match* (1981), on the curling match on the Lake of Monteith when the Bonspiel was held for the first time in sixteen years. It was written by James Wilson, the last Director of Films of Scotland.

Now with a much larger membership, the Committee was led by George Singleton and Andrew Stewart while its film-making effort was co-ordinated with zeal and devotion by Neil Paterson who had agreed to become Director at a crucial stage and who secured valuable contracts from the oil companies. He had the experienced help of Donald Alexander, one of the documentary pioneers of the thirties. There was also always the guidance in administration of Barbara Allan, who was my secretary over the whole of my Directorship and who continued in this capacity under my successor.

When the Committee ceased trading in 1982 the films, all the print material and the bank balance passed into the ownership of the Scottish Film Council, grant-aided by the Scottish Education Department and free of the task of raising money to finance any film-making activities. Thus ended a brave and always well-intentioned endeavour.

After such a comprehensive documentation, it might seem that there could not be many Scottish subjects uncovered. Yet running

49. Associate producer Hugh C. Attwool (left) and Walt Disney, researching *Greyfriars Bobby* (1960).

parallel with Films of Scotland as a source of Scottish films was British Transport Films, where Edgar Anstey, an early associate of John Grierson's, was in charge of production. He maintained an impressive standard in all his films about Scotland. If none of them won an Oscar, as his *Wild Wings* did in 1966, several must have come close to earning that distinction. His films, including those made about Scotland, won awards at many international film festivals.

One of the earliest was *The Heart is Highland* (1952):

From the lone shieling of the misty island
Mountains divide us and the waste of seas;
Yet still the blood is strong, the heart is Highland,
And we in dreams behold the Hebrides.

The film opened with a glimpse of a memorable Edinburgh occasion – The March of the Thousand Pipers in Princes Street. The pipers started out at the Mound eight abreast but, such was the density of the mass of spectators, by the time they had reached the West End they were struggling to get through in single file, with the big drummer at an advantage. If the spectacle was no advertisement for organisation it certainly demonstrated the appeal of massed pipe bands, something the organisers of the Military Tattoo on the Castle Esplanade were to remember. For most of its length the film looked northward to the Highland scene, its survey including whisky distilling, sheep and cattle farming, forestry and hydro-electricity. Several Scottish film-makers had a hand in the film, among them Stewart McAllister, the associate producer, and Cedric Thorpe Davie who wrote the music. Much of its distinctive character derived from Moray McLaren's commentary, spoken with the precision and feeling of a man long familiar with the microphone.

In *Wild Highlands* (1961) the focus was wholly on the wildlife of Scotland. The film followed the flow of the seasons. The first sign of life in the winter wilderness was the raven, feeding its young on carrion. From the tops to the sea-lochs, survivors of winter nurtured another generation: the otter, the heron, the ringed plover, the oyster-catcher and the sandpiper. The film ascended to the high tops in summer, to find the flowers and the grasses and the insects which

132

feed among them. Two thousand feet above the sea the golden eagle hunted to feed its young. The osprey hovered over a loch in search of pike and, successful, flew off on its long haul to the nest in a Scots pine. The film remained in the high tops to find the rutting stags of the wild red deer – a sequence which alone would have made *Wild Highlands* memorable. John Buxton carried out the research and collaborated with Ronald Craigen in the photography.

If it covered familiar ground, *Scotland for Sport* (1958) did so with enterprise. The Clyde was the main focus for yachting, seen against the splendour of the hills surrounding the estuary. The Tay at Aberfeldy was the setting for the extraordinary canoeing sequence. For climbing the film moved to the Cuillins in Skye – astonishing vistas of remote, sinister, jagged mountains. Golf at St Andrews, skiing in the Cairngorms, fishing in the lochs and rivers, pony trekking in the hills. Ian Ferguson and Kenneth Fairbairn collaborated in the production and the commentary was written and spoken by Alastair Borthwick, in his day as well-known in Scotland for his voice as for his writing.

In some of the films the promotional purpose was more self-conscious than in others, although the colour photography of the Scottish landscape always gave pleasure. *Coasts of Clyde* (1959) had Bernard Braden travelling by train and steamer to the isle of Arran whence his grandmother had sailed for the New World. *Golfers in a Scottish Landscape* (1971) visited some of the country's best known courses, where Antonia Fraser's biography of Mary Stuart appeared incongruously to be required reading. *Next Stop Scotland* (1968) described the motoring holidays of two married couples, one young and adventurously driving a vintage car and the other dignified and decorous in an estate car: the central Highlands and the Clyde for the young people, Skye and the Outer Hebrides for the other visitors. The commentary, in different voices, embraced everything a visitor would want to know about the country.

Several of the British Transport films – understandably, given their purpose – had a regional basis. They were designed to invite tourist visitation. *Sing of the Border* (1964) succeeded both in doing that and in being an imaginative film by any standard. It used as a framework the stirring songs of the Border country, which

50. James Kennaway's first novel *Tunes of Glory* became a film (1960) with a plot as sharp and unrelenting as open warfare, reaching its climax in an outburst of neurotic rage. Left to right: Duncan Macrae, John Mills, Alec Guinness and Gordon Jackson.

51. Maggie Smith (centre) with her 'set' in *The Prime of Miss Jean Brodie* (1968): still the classic film of Edinburgh. The crème de la crème, left to right: Jane Carr, Pamela Franklin, Diane Grayson, Shirley Steedman.

told the story of the area, and blended them with the contemporary scene to provide a counterpoint in sound and picture. The annual burning of whin bushes, a familiar spring spectacle in the Borders, was used to great effect in suggesting the warring raids from the south. Ian Wallace and Rory McEwen were among the singers. Begun by Tony Thompson the film was completed after his death by Kenneth Fairbairn and Muir Mathieson, who spoke the commentary. Mathieson's name as composer was on dozens of films made in or about Scotland. Inspiration never seemed to fail him. I have a memory of him playing over on the piano in Basil Wright's house in Oxfordshire the music he had composed and would later conduct for *The Line to Skye*. His considerable contribution to Scottish film-making should be on record.

Glasgow Belongs to Me (1966), produced for Anstey by IFA (Scotland) with direction by Laurence Henson and photography by Edward McConnell, had both affection for its subject and wit in its treatment. The film traced how what in the days of Daniel Defoe was 'the beautifullest little city I have seen in Britain' grew into a thriving metropolis, in the early eighteenth century enriched by the tobacco trade, holding for a time the proud title of 'second city of Empire' and, despite its slums, containing some of the finest building of the Victorian period. It captured the spirit of Will Fyffe's song 'I Belong to Glasgow', with the city going round and round from the air, and if the sequence on football was inevitable its treatment was ingenious. McConnell used to good effect the models of steam engines and ships in the Kelvingrove Museum. I included the film in a 'Scotland on the Screen' programme taken overseas, and could always gauge the number of Glasgow-born people in the audience by their response to the shot of a housewife in the Gorbals enjoying 'a guid hing oot': silence in Ottawa, an immediate burst of laughter in Hamilton.

British Transport were among the sponsors of *A Line for All Seasons* (1981), also produced by IFA (Scotland) and directed and photographed by Eddie McConnell. In it the cameraman turned his magical eye on the seasonal beauty that awaits the traveller on the West Highland Railway, where the landscape from the moving train can be as spectacular in the middle of winter as in the height of summer. He did not restrict himself to the route of the railway and introduced some stunning shots of his favourite Loch Lomond. The film also incorporated the story of a stubborn landscape, conquered by an equally stubborn band of railway engineers who, immersed in the Victorian railway fever, pressed on against great difficulties. The line, which runs from Glasgow to Fort William and the west coast port of Mallaig, exemplifies in the splendid viaduct at Glenfinnan the first use of the then new building material, mass concrete. Though derided by traditionalist ironmasters with the nickname 'Concrete Bob', the pioneering Robert McAlpine attracted the attention of engineers everywhere to the West Highland and its innovative construction. This McConnell was able to convey in a film of sustained beauty.

Of all the British Transport's Scottish films, none made a deeper impression than *The Land of Robert Burns* (1956). When Anstey first approached me about this film I suggested that the treatment might be written by Maurice Lindsay, acknowledged authority on the poet's life and work. The film was produced by Stewart McAllister, former member of the GPO Film Unit and a Scot familiar with the poet's background. He left his stamp on the film by also speaking the commentary. When the film was shown at the 1956 Edinburgh Film Festival John Grierson paid a tribute to McAllister which is worth hearing again since it is so relevant to the theme of this book:

> The sad thing about Burns in Scotland is that so many have had a go at him and few have ever been greatly pleased with the result. Partly it is because nothing can ever quite come up to scratch when you are dealing with a national myth. Partly it is because Burns is at root a controversial figure. Some are not much interested in his so-called sins and think his affairs exaggerated and his drinking just incompetent. Some again are not even sure of him as a poet, when it comes to consideration of the longer wind. They allow *Tam o'Shanter* and much that was rich and roaring when it was good eighteenth century satirical stuff but shy at the lines that got away to a wonderful start and never far thereafter. Some even have thought him a love poet only in the domain of artifice and convention.

52. In *Mary, Queen of Scots* (1972), Vanessa Redgrave tried to make a positive figure of Mary and gave her some convincing moments, but the inconsistencies in the Queen's record defeated her.

In the circumstances it is a brave thing to do a Burns film at all and what is odd is that the way through the brickbats has been so easy after all. I think Stewart McAllister just walked on the water and was done with it. He trusted rightly to the landscape to evoke what Burns was talking about; and it was so lovely in itself that there was no harm at all in giving Burns not only the credit of it but the copyright of it too. Then again he re-enacted nothing to embarrass you with reminder of what romantic liars your parents were. The girls among the corn rigs were by an odd act of simple genius just what they looked to be, buxom and blest in it as you or I – never mind Burns – could have wished for.

It may be that the *Cotter's Saturday Night* sits a little heavily on McAllister. There is, here and there, homely get together and an ominous word of prayer but one's decent feeling is that it is not so much remembered from Burns – where it was false – as from McAllister's old man – where it was probably genuine.

Best deviation of all is the fact that the lovers' lane note is struck exclusively in longshot. It is not just a question of relieving you of the gratuitous and inadequate intrusion of the cinema into poetic imagery; it is simply a question of letting Afton for a sweet change flow as softly as the poet so specifically instructs. It is true we once used it otherwise. We had them sing it in *The Brave Don't Cry* when the miners below were about to die. Maybe you thought it dramatic and even sentimental that they should be thinking of such pure things then. Hell, the Afton was the dirty burn flowing through the bings above them at Knockshinnoch and the water that was killing them. It doesn't alter the point that Afton – longshot and upriver – saved the day for Burns.

The Burns film in short has the great integrity of being what one honest fellow thinks Burns to be. It rests wisely on the countryside that bore him and blest him, and blesses us the more today for the voice it gave him. The film evokes the poet in time as you might find him today if you could get down to the river again or to the Spring again rightly and as you should.

It is not about my love is like a red, red rose which is possibly a more passionate concept than McAllister might think it seemly to indulge – and I am not sure he isn't right. It is only about the banks and braes that bloom and are bonnie before worse, sometimes all too sentimentally and melodramatically, befalls. That I find fair enough as not only within the competence of the cinema to do well but in this case to do with a quite moving sincerity. Better I say good McAllister than bad Burns – and this is Cavalcanti's favourite editor and my own favourite, if ever innocent, Burns-lover at his best.

About this time there was a proposal in Hollywood that Bing Crosby should appear as Burns in a film. That affront at least we were saved.

8

After Brigadoon

In the post-*Brigadoon* decades there was a strong sense of *déjà-vu* about Scottish feature film-making: three or four *Macbeths*, new versions of *The Thirty-Nine Steps*, *Kidnapped* and *Whisky (Rockets) Galore!*, another *Mary Queen of Scots*, even a *Return to the Edge of the World*. Had the film writers run out of ideas? Or did the film-makers want to improve on past failures? There was still an over-riding tendency to make adaptations of books and plays and not enough writing direct for the screen. The reason was largely economic. It seemed less of a financial gamble to base a film on something introduced and popularised in another medium.

This was most obviously the case with the various *Macbeths*. Shakespeare had laid the foundation with a solid drama, based on his own version of history, with a beginning, a middle and an end, a touch of the supernatural and enough bloody deeds to satisfy audiences, familiar to sudden death through the gangster movies. There was always curiosity to see what a director had made of Shakespeare's tale.

Orson Welles made his *Macbeth* in 1948 although several years were to pass before it reached Britain. He had long cherished the idea and had tried to interest several companies. Eventually he was able to persuade Republic Pictures, a modest Hollywood company, for which he was later to make the farcical *Trouble in the Glen* in Scotland, to undertake the production. It was shot in three weeks. There was no producer to restrain Welles in his excesses: everything was darker or larger or bloodier or more violent than in the original of which very little of the text, ruthlessly mauled, remained. He introduced an additional character, a Holy Father, and gave him lines from other characters in the play. His Macbeth was personally involved in the slaughter of Lady Macduff and her children. He roused Lady Macbeth from her sleep-walking and had her end her life by throwing herself over a cliff. Throughout the film the action was dominated by a magnified Macbeth, seen as a huge menacing figure in the foreground of nearly every shot.

Welles maintained later that he had made the film according to his own conception of Macbeth: 'He was a detestable man until he became king, and then once he is crowned he is doomed; but once he is doomed he becomes a great man.' If this were indeed his interpretation it would have needed a more skilful performance to convey it. His acting lacked control, was indulgently exaggerated. In New York he had had the experienced help of the Mercury Theatre players but here little known actors had few opportunities to register and could not turn to Shakespeare for help in their characterisation.

Can anything be said in favour of this *Macbeth*? Perhaps the determination of the director to give it a cinematic form. Penelope Houston wrote that the 'remarkable thing is the quantity of sheer power, melodramatic grandeur and intellectual feeling about the play that does come through'. It made its impact through the Welles performance and by the conception of a primitive Scotland, inhabited by vicious, ruthless and superstitious warriors. The art director, Fred Ritter, had been instructed to keep everything as dark and dank as possible and in this he was entirely successful. No glint of sunshine illumined the gloom. The film had little significance for Scotland. Had the treatment been more restrained and responsible it might have had the quality of Grigori Kosintsev's *Hamlet*, where the play survived the editing of Shakespeare's verse.

The Japanese director, Akira Kurosawa, was to make the most memorable *Macbeth* adaptation, *Kumonosu-ja (Throne of Blood)* (1957), although its outstanding achievement relates only incidentally to the subject of this book. Here the theme was re-interpreted by a master film-maker who did not need to display violence to achieve impact and could command suspense through visual imagination. A film of *Macbeth* made in Scotland would need a director of comparable stature to justify itself.

Cinematically George Schaefer's *Macbeth* (1961) was the least ambitious, the most content to be a record of a stage performance.

53. Nigel Havers (left) and Ian Charleson as Eric Liddell in Hugh Hudson's
Oscar-winning *Chariots of Fire* (1981). It was a well-timed film, arriving
when world interest in international sport was in the ascendancy, and
a worthy tribute to Liddell himself.

There were some effective exteriors, including a shot of Macbeth and Banquo riding across a genuine Scottish landscape. For the most part, however, its interest lay in the performances of Maurice Evans and Judith Anderson, created for the stage and retaining the flavour of the theatre. Their acting was sincere and, within the theatrical convention, effective. Evans suggested a deeply troubled man with a mind 'full of scorpions' while Judith Anderson skilfully judged Lady Macbeth's descent into madness. In contrast to the experience of Orson Welles, they were well supported, especially by Ian Bannen as Macduff but also by players who knew how to give Shakespeare's poetry maximum impact: Michael Hordern as Banquo, Felix Aylmer as the doctor and Malcolm Keen as Duncan. The use of location shots as backgrounds for studio action was awkwardly accomplished and did not contribute to the unity of the film.

Roman Polanski's *Macbeth* (1972) had at least as much violence as the Welles version although here the director, it was generally believed, was responding to the murder in Hollywood, while he was in London, of his pregnant wife, Sharon Tate, and several of their friends. It was not his first indulgence in violence but he seemed to be taking a kind of vengeance in the bloodbath scenes. In the writing of the treatment Polanski collaborated with Kenneth Tynan, his main objective being to turn into visual images the parts of the play related to action which could not be shown on the stage, including the violent murder of Lady Macduff and her children and the decapitation of Macbeth. The writers wanted to cast young players in the main parts, which they felt would give plausibility to the theme of ambition. Polanski chose Jon Finch, then twenty-eight, and as Lady Macbeth Francesca Annis, who had played Ophelia in Nicol Williamson's *Hamlet* in New York. It was decided that she would be in the nude in the sleep-walking scene, on the theory that there were no nightgowns in Macbeth's time. So the writers rationalised something in accordance with their separate reputations.

Interior shooting – over twenty-five weeks – was done at Shepperton. For the exteriors Polanski and Tynan perversely chose the Snowdonia National Park, where the unit survived

144

a month of atrocious weather, and Lindisfarne and Bamburgh castles, both wrong in period and much too grand for Macbeth's Scotland. In the studio Polanski took excessive care over detail: it was said that he would spend three hours getting a candle to flicker to his satisfaction. He imposed his own interpretation on the players. The film was $600,000 over its budget of $2,400,000 and behind on schedule when it was eventually rescued by Hugh Hefner of *Playboy*.

When it emerged in February 1972, the pressures on Polanski at the time of its production were inevitably recalled and comparisons drawn between the murder of his wife and friends and the grim events of the play. This was unfair to Polanski who was not involved in any way with what happened in his Hollywood home while he was working in London. Nevertheless his preoccupation with bloody detail was excessive. 'No chance to revel in gore is passed up' wrote one critic, reflecting a general response. It is strange that a director who could indulge in so much violence in adapting *Macbeth* should, a few years later, show a studied and sustained restraint in making *Tess* when the opportunity for exploiting sexual violence was at least as great.

Another Scottish literary subject, much milked over a long period, was Stevenson's short story, *Dr Jekyll and Mr Hyde*. One of the earliest, as a sound film, was the version made with that title in Hollywood by Paramount in 1932. It was directed by Rouben Mamoulian and had in high degree the imaginative qualities which distinguished his work. According to the critic Ephraim Katz, it remains famous for its use of the subjective camera, for its dramatic light-and-shadow effects, for its frightening on-camera transformation of Fredric March from Dr Jekyll to Mr Hyde, for the performances of March and of Miriam Hopkins as the trollop and for its intelligent emphasis on emotion and sexual tension. The Edinburgh setting was not much in evidence although the period sense was strong.

The story continued to be filmed and re-filmed over the years. It passed from Paramount to Metro-Goldwyn-Mayer whose version, directed by Victor Fleming in 1941, had Spencer Tracy and Ingrid Bergman in the leading parts. Tracy had been reluctant to become

145

involved: the need to portray the evil living within Dr Jekyll did not accord with the conception of himself as a warm, responsive person. Ingrid Bergman, under contract to David Selznick, had been cast as the fiancée and not the barmaid but she balked at the prospect of being type-cast as a sweet-natured heroine. After a secret test with the director she was given the part she wanted. It changed her life. 'Never have I given myself so completely', she wrote in *My Life*. 'For the first time I have broken out from the cage which encloses me, and opened a shutter to the outside world'. Ingrid Bergman's performance was successful because she was determined to prove herself as an actress. Tracy's was less convincing, something of the unease he felt coming over on the screen. Victor Fleming's direction had the assurance expected from one of Hollywood's most reliable film-makers.

Several adaptations still lay ahead. *The Body Snatcher* (1945) was directed by Robert Wise with Val Lewton as producer, a highly successful collaboration. Wise, who edited *Citizen Kane* and *The Magnificent Ambersons* for Orson Welles, turned this version of the Stevenson story into 'a subtle philosophical disquisition on the nature of good and evil'. Boris Karloff played the grave-digger for the anatomy classes, the lugubrious Henry Daniell the surgeon and Bela Lugosi was the foreigner, haunting the streets for young girls. They made a sinister trio! The director's Edinburgh, subtly suggested by the cameraman, Robert De Grasse, was a patchwork, strongest in its image of the castle emerging from the mists of a dark and dreich city. A version with many imaginative touches.

The Flesh and the Fiends (1950), directed by John Gilling, thought of itself as 'the story of lost men and lost souls . . . vice and murder'. It was probably the most straightforward telling of the story. It had Peter Cushing as Dr Knox, Donald Pleasence as Hare, George Rose as Burke and parts for Dermot Walsh, Renée Houston, Billie Whitelaw and John Cairney. *Burke and Hare* (1971), directed by Vernon Sewell, demonstrated the undiminishing fascination the subject held for film-makers. Harry Andrews played Dr Knox and Derren Nesbitt and Glynn Edwards Burke and Hare. The film had an Edinburgh première before an audience drawn from the medical world. They were more embarrassed than impressed when they left.

54. Steven Archibald in Bill Douglas's *My Childhood* (1972): playing truant in Edinburgh on the day the director ran into him.

Hammer's *Dr Jekyll and Sister Hyde* (1971), directed by Roy Ward Baker, had Dr Jekyll (Ralph Bates) discovering that female hormones could be a transforming elixir and, experimenting on himself, he becomes a young and beautiful woman. Burke and Hare provide him with the corpses. The transformation sequences were astonishing and while the film was unmistakable Hammer in style, actor, director and cameraman, Norman Warwick, made it always something more than a gimmick.

Its origin made *The Doctor and the Devils* (1985) one of the more interesting versions of the story. Donald Taylor of the Strand Film Company (Grierson's brother-in-law) wrote a story about Dr Knox involving much research (including the fact that Knox served as a doctor at Waterloo when Burke acted as medical orderly in the same battle). He commissioned Dylan Thomas, then working for him, to write a screenplay, published in 1957. It had to wait until 1985 to be made into a film, although a stage version was presented at the Edinburgh Festival. The film was not, however, made in Edinburgh as I am sure the documentary-trained Taylor would have wished. It was made at Shepperton Studios: 'A reproduction of an 1830s English (*sic*) market square, it reeks with atmosphere. And with pools of dirty water on cobbled streets, assorted livestock, 150 extras in tatty garb and various quantities of organic debris dressing the scene, it even smells authentic'. The film was produced by Jonathan Sanger and directed by Freddie Francis (he made thirty horror films for Hammer); Timothy Dalton played the anatomist, Jonathan Pryce and Stephen Rae the body-snatchers and the cast included Twiggy, Beryl Reid and Phyllis Logan. Donald Taylor had a serious purpose in writing his story and wanted to reveal how much Knox had contributed to anatomical science but who is remembered today only because his name is linked to two murderers. The serious purpose did not survive the much delayed realisation of the film project.

There was much re-assembling of talents for *Rockets Galore!* (1958): production by Basil Dearden, direction by Michael Relph (both formerly of Ealing), scenario by Monja Danischewsky, from the novel by Compton Mackenzie. The conflict between rebellious natives and interfering bureaucrats had not changed much either, except that

148

here they were not trying to prevent illegal salvaging of whisky but attempting to convert Todday into a rocket base. The bureaucrats are circumvented by an Ealing-like device, the painting of all the seagulls pink so that they come under the protection of bird-lovers as a rare species. Danischewsky knew the location and also how to make the most of the situation, perhaps adding a little here and there of his bubbling sense of humour. In the home team were all the regulars – Duncan Macrae, Jameson Clark, Gordon Jackson and Jean Cadell – while the visitors included Donald Sinden, Roland Culver, Ian Hunter and Catherine Lacey. The outcome was never in doubt. Perhaps everyone concerned knew that while you could remake *Whisky Galore!* you could not command success for it.

So too with the new version of *The Thirty-Nine Steps* (1960). To realise just how much was lost from the original it is worth recalling a tribute once paid in a broadcast by a fellow Scot, Walter Elliot, who also knew how to use words:

> He could write about the small, hidden, green valleys of the Border till they closed round you; he could write of journeys, breathless, cross-country, perilous, till your breath came short and your heart hammered on your ribs. He could produce the totally unexpected – the true story-teller's jewel – time after time with no more than a flick of the wrist. However often we read it, we shall always be thrilled by the moment in *The Thirty-Nine Steps* when Dick Hannay, African mining engineer, locked up in Kirkcudbrightshire, identifies the small square slabs in a corner of his cellar as blasting explosive, and realises that he has the professional knowledge and skill to lay a charge just strong enough to blow the wall away and let him free, and no more. There was that gusto about Buchan's work which, when he got going, hurried you along like a high wind.

Little of that gusto remained in Ralph Thomas's film. There was none of the sense of impending world events which was so important in the story as Buchan conceived it. No one took very seriously the murders and the conspiracies and even the escape from the train crossing the Forth Bridge had lost its edge through familiarity. Kenneth More's characterisation of Hannay was light-hearted, in accordance with the mood of the film. Of the attachment of Tania

55. Steven Archibald again in *My Ain Folk* (1973): the young Jamie soon realises that he is unloved and unwanted.

56. *My Ain Folk* (1973): an unremittingly honest portrayal of a deprived childhood, the trilogy stands above and apart from any other Scottish film.

Elg to More by handcuff and having to spend the night with her, John Grierson found that 'the alien menace to our island home is well forgotten in the arch and gamey innuendos of the situation'. The crofter's cottage of the Hitchcock version became here a small Highland hotel with Brenda de Banzie as a sex-mad old crystal gazer and Reginald Beckwith as her poor cuckolded husband. Was it worth the effort to turn the Buchan story into a lightweight frolic?

More echoes in *The Bridal Path* (1959). With the popular success of *Geordie* on record, Frank Launder and Sidney Gilliat asked me if I could find a story with the same elements. If it succeeded I could have the credit and, if it failed, the blame. I read, or reread, a number of novels and eventually suggested *The Bridal Path* by Nigel Trantor, an author with a good track record in undemanding actionful narrative. The central situation concerned the threat of consanguinity (the marrying of first cousins) on a small Hebridean island, from which a widower with two small children is sent to the mainland to find a wife. The elders give him a list of instructions which include a ban on any girl from the Clan Campbell (a reflection of hostility dating from the Massacre of Glencoe). There are inevitable complications and a neat twist in the tail. It would never have made an epic, as Launder and Gilliat must have known. Bill Travers gave the hero a likeable naïveté, the strong Scottish cast included Gordon Jackson, Duncan Macrae and Alex Mackenzie and there were songs from the Campbeltown Gaelic Choir to accompany the wifeless islander as he tramped over the hills. Arthur Ibbetson photographed the Highland landscape and Cedric Thorpe Davie arranged the music. I did not hear again from the producers.

Monja Danischewsky returned to Scotland to make *Battle of the Sexes* (1959), as big a contrast as could be imagined to his Hebridean films. According to Charles Crichton, the director, introducing the film at the 1988 Edinburgh Film Festival, Danischewsky's version was the sixth re-writing of the short story by James Thurber, 'The Catbird Seat', on which it was based. The setting was contemporary Edinburgh and the theme the disturbing impact on an old-established tweed firm of a young American woman efficiency expert. Standing firm against any tinkering with tradition is a little, middle-aged clerk who sabotages the system and, when the staff is dismissed and the firm adopts synthetic fibre, plots first to murder the woman and then to have her certified as insane.

The strength of the film lay in the performance of Peter Sellers as the stubborn traditionalist. With his finely attuned ear he had adopted the Edinburgh accent to the last inflection. On and off the set he spoke in the same way. I recall lunching with him during the making of the film and thinking, 'He speaks just like my father!' Efforts during luncheon to get him to drop the tonal disguise were unavailing. In London he had heard about the film in advance and phoned his offer to play the part out of the blue. Danischewsky thought it was a brilliant bit of casting – which it was – and that the film helped to put Sellers at the head of his profession. Robert Morley played the tweed shop proprietor and Constance Cummings the American who found him susceptible to her arguments for change. The contributions of Jameson Clark, Moultrie Kelsall, Alex Mackenzie, Roddy Macmillan and James Gibson helped the Scottish atmosphere. James Thurber, despite his impaired eyesight, saw the film in New York and wrote to Danischewsky to congratulate him on it. 'Everyone with us seemed to like the film as much as we did'.

I have another memory of the film which, in its small way, is revealing. Danischewsky asked me to find a shop front, preferably in George Street, which would suggest solidity and respect for tradition. We settled on the pillared portico of Blackwood's, the old established publishing house. The head of the firm agreed but Danischewsky was told that they always closed at 5 p.m. and shooting would need to be completed by then. Almost inevitably the unit, with all its paraphernalia, was late in arriving. In refusing admission the proprietor was as adamant as Robert Morley's character was in the film – a nice comment on the inflexibility of tradition.

Walt Disney's experience in making *Rob Roy* had been sufficiently rewarding to bring him back to Scotland on several occasions in the sixties. Expectations were never very high, but nevertheless more devoted effort went into the films than might have been expected from a company whose target was popular entertainment.

There was a hint of this devotion in a thirty-minute travel film made in 1957 for the 'People and Places' series. When the content of *Scotland* was being discussed I was astonished to be told that there were to be no motor-cars in the film: 'Nothing dates more quickly than a motor-car, and we want the film to be in circulation for years'. And so the unit went off to Lewis to film a sale of cattle at an isolated road junction, a hand-shake concluding the deal. The fishermen cast their nets and the womenfolk spun their wool. There was a visit to Abbotsford, home of Sir Walter Scott, and another to a children's Hallowe'en party. Nothing untoward happened to distort the impression of a picturesque land and a people living in the past. Geoffrey Foot directed.

Walt Disney's British company returned in 1959 to make a version of *Kidnapped*. They were well prepared. Robert Stevenson, who directed, had also written the scenario and had remained remarkably faithful to the original. He had also assembled an excellent cast. Peter Finch was a convincingly swashbuckling Alan Breck and James MacArthur a sturdy David Balfour. But the distinctive character of the film derived mainly from the Scottish players. John Laurie had one of his most rewarding parts as Ebenezer Balfour and the others included Finlay Currie – a source of strength in any film – Duncan Macrae, Andrew Cruickshank, Alex Mackenzie, Jack Stewart and Abe Barker. Add Niall MacGinnis, Peter O'Toole and Miles Malleson and the film would have needed ham-fisted direction to fail. The film moved through some of Scotland's most spectacular scenery, shot by Paul Beeson with real affection. Cedric Thorpe Davie's music was played under the direction of Muir Mathieson, two Scots whose names on a film meant much pleasure for the ear.

Greyfriars Bobby (1960), given Disney's interest in animals, was inevitable. Here again the intentions were good. I accompanied an associate producer who was sent to Edinburgh to survey locations. There were too many television aerials on the houses adjoining Greyfriars Church for the kirkyard to be used as a background; and the farm on the southern approaches to the city, another authentic location, had been so modernised that it clearly did not have the right atmosphere. So the story of a dog's faithfulness to his master enduring for fourteen years after his death had to be filmed in the studios. A brave effort was made by the director, Don Chaffey, to

57. Steven Archibald in *My Way Home* (1978): Jamie begins to come to terms with himself and to leave behind his self-pitying, dissatisfied adolescence.

keep sentimentality in check; but how can you do this with such characters as John Brown (Donald Crisp) and Mr Traill (Laurence Naismith), not to mention the dog? Some tension was developed in the courtroom scene, with Moultrie Kelsall's stern magistrate in the chair – tension which was resolved when Andrew Cruickshank's kind-hearted Lord Provost granted the dog the Freedom of the City. Alex Mackenzie, Gordon Jackson, Duncan Macrae amd Jameson Clark were there (and how often they were called on!) to add an authentic flavour to the characterisation.

In the same tradition, but with a cat as the central figure, was *The Three Lives of Thomasina* (1963), adapted by Robert Westerby from the novel by Paul Gallico, again with Don Chaffey as director. Here the setting was Inverary, spurned for *Brigadoon*, the studio work being completed at Pinewood. Thomasina has to be destroyed because she has tetanus; but the business is bungled by the vet's assistant and the cat survives. The situation is productive of maximum sentimentality, compounded by the reaction of the children. There was even a touch of Disney fantasy when Thomasina believes herself dead and finds herself in a Cat Heaven, with an Egyptian Cat Goddess and Siamese cats in attendance. Susan Hampshire played the girl who lives in the woods and has a way with animals, while Patrick McGoohan gave authority to his part as the vet. Finlay Currie was again in the cast and there was a part for Jean Anderson.

Jack Couffer, who worked for many years on Disney's wildlife films, came to Scotland to direct *Ring of Bright Water* (1969), based on Gavin Maxwell's book about his life with the otters at his West Highland cottage, Camusfearna. It was produced by Joseph Strick, whose rawly realistic film *The Savage Eye* was the sensation of the Edinburgh Film Festival of 1959 and who also made an equally controversial film of James Joyce's *Ulysses*. *Ring of Bright Water* was a new departure for an always imaginative film-maker.

In outline the story was simple enough: an association which develops between a writer, eager to escape from the pressures of life in London, and an otter he buys in a petshop and takes with him to an 'ideal retreat' in the West Highlands. The film becomes a daily chronicle of the intermingled lives of man and animal, one finding a friendly response in a neighbouring woman doctor and the other wandering off to look for a mate. Despite the brutal killing of the otter by a road workman who thinks it is an outsize rat there is a happy ending. Couffer brought all his Disney experience to the filming of the otter, a natural for a sympathetic camera. The story had been adapted by Bill Travers, working with the director, and he was joined in front of the camera by Virginia McKenna, renewing their association in the making of the film about lions in Kenya, *Born Free*. Their enthusiasm for the subject showed in the film, a magical blending of Highland scenery and human involvement in animal freedom. Archie Duncan had the unenviable part of the roadmender and elsewhere there were brief appearances for such excellent Scottish players as Roddy Macmillan, Jameson Clark, Jean Taylor-Smith, Helena Gloag and James Gibson. A modest and enjoyable film.

During this period of film-making there were several Scottish films which were substantially different in theme, even if they had originated in another medium. One was *Tunes of Glory* (1960), adapted from the novel by James Kennaway. It was his first novel, highly successful on publication and full of promise for its author, then only twenty-eight. He entered film-making under the best possible auspices – Sir Michael Balcon's Ealing Studios where he had Sandy Mackendrick, Monja Danischewsky and Pat Tennyson as associates. His first original script, *Violent Playground* (1958), directed by Basil Dearden, dealt with juvenile delinquency against the background of high-rise urban development in Liverpool. For Michael Relph, another Ealing producer, he had begun work on a screen adaptation of *Tunes of Glory* in 1957; but, after endless discussion about the advisability of making a film on a military subject, especially in the post-Suez atmosphere, and the involvement as advisers of Mackendrick and Kenneth Tynan, Ealing went cold on the project. Kennaway was beginning to experience the frustrations of trying to work creatively in films.

Eventually – he was under contract to Rank – the project resurfaced, with Colin Lesslie as producer and, as director, Ronald Neame, who had on record such films as *Brief Encounter* and *Great Expectations*. The intention was to shoot the film at Stirling Castle,

58. In the sculpture gallery at Newby Hall, from *The Hand of Adam*, directed by Murray Grigor (1975).

59. Shooting the climax of *The Great Mill Race* (1975), directed by Robin Crichton (seen in rear, centre).

the regimental headquarters of the Argyll and Sutherland Highlanders – a spectacular setting strong in atmosphere, with a significance for Scots everywhere. But the War Office had doubts: the army was presented in a critical light and this was not their conception of how an officers' mess should be shown. In the compromise reached the soldiers provided for the film were Irish Guardsmen, the tartan was unidentifiable and Stirling Castle became a studio set (and a very convincing one by Wilfred Shingleton).

Like all good films, *Tunes of Glory* embodied a conflict: between a martinet of a commanding officer, all for discipline and efficiency, and his immediate predecessor, easy-going, hard-drinking, magnet for the loyalty of most of the members of the mess. The conflict followed a course as sharp and unrelenting as open warfare, reaching its climax in an outburst of neurotic rage by the commanding officer at a regimental cocktail party, and a subsequent incident when a soldier is struck in public by his former commanding officer. Both contestants invited some sympathy, which fortified the appeal of the film. Suicide for one and descent into madness for the other produced a conclusion typical of the film's toughness.

John Mills gave the more convincing performance as an officer determined to do his duty as he saw it and who gradually cracked under the strain. Alec Guinness, hampered by an uncertain Scottish accent, had his moments, especially in his final confrontation and in all his scenes with Gordon Jackson. Dennis Price as the major responsive to the new man, Duncan Macrae as the pipe-major and John Fraser as the piper all contributed performances which, under Neame's firm direction, gave the film an extra interest for its character studies. *Tunes of Glory* had a long-running success in Britain, the United States and the Commonwealth. It continues to appear regularly on television. Kennaway's script was one of the five nominations for an Oscar as Best Screenplay from Another Medium in 1960, the award going to Richard Brooks for *Elmer Gantry*.

James Kennaway's death in a car accident in 1968 was more than conventionally tragic. He had already shown enough talent in his writing for the stage and screen to suggest that he might have given Scottish film-making what, since the retirement of Neil Paterson, it badly needed: a script writer accepted in both Britain and Hollywood. His death occurred before *Country Dance* (1969), based on his play which in turn was adapted from his novel *Household Ghosts*, went into production. It was unsuccessful as a play. J. Lee Thompson, who directed the film, was in disagreement with Peter O'Toole over the interpretation of the leading part and claimed that the difficulties might have been overcome had Kennaway been directly involved.

Country Dance drew on Kennaway's familiarity with rural Perthshire and the social mores of the area. His intention, according to his biographer Trevor Royle, was to write about 'a closely-knit family whose past ghosts return to haunt them and to dominate their actions at a time of great stress'. Novel and screenplay passed through several rewritings and what emerged in the film was lacking in structure and clarity. O'Toole's character was a wild-eyed gentleman farmer, living with the estranged wife (Susannah York) of a former employee, now successfully managing a neighbouring farm. At a Young Conservatives' country dance the tensions surface and partners in passion change disconcertingly. The climax, which sees the O'Toole character dispatched to a mental home, does not seem to be an adequate resolution of the complicated interrelationship. The large cast included several Scottish players such as Robert Urquhart, Lennox Milne, Jean Anderson, Helena Gloag, Madeleine Christie and Leonard Maguire. Some exteriors were shot in Strathearn and the film was completed at the Ardmore Studios at Bray in Ireland. In contrast to the solid achievement of *Tunes of Glory*, *Country Dance* made little impact, even when given a prestige screening at the Edinburgh Film Festival in 1970.

There are two footnotes to the Kennaway film story which should go on record. In April 1970 the Scottish Arts Council, 'as small recognition on our part of his very important contribution in the two fields of literature and film', announced a screenplay competition in his honour. Contributions were invited for a thirty-minute script. The judges, Bruce Beresford, Murray Grigor and Neil Paterson, did not find any single entry worthy of the prize of £500 and the award was divided between three writers. Perhaps it came too early in the Scottish film renaissance: the documentary film-makers were just beginning to turn their attention to story films. Today a similar competition would surely produce more filmable ideas.

Some ten years later a short story of Kennaway's did become a successful thirty-minute film. This was *The Dollar Bottom* (1980), set in Glenalmond in Perthshire, the boarding school where Kennaway was educated. It concerned an insurance scheme devised by one of the pupils to offer protection against beatings. Those who knew the school and Kennaway's contemporaries well recognised both the setting and pupils and enjoyed the joke when they read the story and later saw the film. Unhappily the school governors did not share this reaction and the film was shot, not at Glenalmond but in Edinburgh, at Cargilfield and Fettes, with boys from Daniel Stewart's-Melville College and from the Scottish Youth Theatre. Robert Urquhart played the headmaster. The house master was played by Rikki Fulton, an actor whose capacity for mime, comparable to Fernandel and Jacques Tati, remains strangely unexploited in films. Roger Christian directed. In 1981 *The Dollar Bottom* received an Oscar in Hollywood as the Best Short Fiction Film.

There are obvious links between *Tunes of Glory* and the other substantial film of the period, *The Prime of Miss Jean Brodie* (1968). Both were originally novels, both are based on conflicts between determined characters, and both were directed by Ronald Neame. Muriel Spark's novella had already appeared as a play by Jay Presson Allen and film followed play fairly closely. What we saw was not an attempt to capture the ironic subtleties of the Spark original but rather a film about a teacher who believed, 'Give me a girl at an impressionable age and she is mine for life'.

The school at which she taught (James Gillespie's in Edinburgh) was typical of several tight-knit educational institutions in the city where the discipline imposed by the headmistress could be as unrelenting as in James Kennaway's regiment. In this sense the film had something in common with Leontine Sagan's *Maedchen in Uniform*. There were, until very recently, such schools in Edinburgh and several generations of schoolgirls would recognise themselves in Miss Brodie's pupils.

In the film Miss Brodie discards the prescribed curriculum, enthuses about the rich discoveries to be made in European art

60. **Burt Lancaster and Fulton Mackay in Bill Forsyth's** *Local Hero* (1983): in part a riposte to *Brigadoon,* and a step in the tradition of *I Know Where I'm Going.*

and, more controversially, finds much to admire in the activities of Franco and Mussolini. Her other eccentricity, perhaps not so unusual, is to pamper her favourite pupils. There are involvements of different kinds with the art master and the music master and eventually a confrontation with the headmistress who tries to force her to resign. When she is denounced by a pupil and is dismissed, the little world she has created falls apart and the pupils are stranded. Or are they? The film does not carry them beyond the classroom.

Much of the appeal of the film lay in the performance of Maggie Smith. She used all her formidable theatrical skill to bring Jean Brodie to life, and as she was seldom off the screen she dominated the action. Celia Johnson as the disapproving headmistress was a credible creation and the scenes between them, Miss Brodie cool and confident, the other striving to assert her authority, were high in drama. As was his habit, Neame had assembled a strong cast, including Robert Stephens as the art master with a roving eye, Gordon Jackson as the upright music master, and Pamela Franklin as the precocious pupil. Exteriors for the film were shot at a Glasgow school but the Edinburgh ambience was still unmistakable.

It might have helped if *Mary, Queen of Scots* (1972) had had an identifiable Edinburgh setting. Instead, the use of Bamburgh Castle for Holyrood deprived the film of credibility, at least for those (not limited to Scots) who knew that the restored solid battlements of the spacious Northumbrian building had nothing in common with the compact turreted palace at the foot of the Royal Mile.

The timespan of the film was rather more extensive than in some of the other versions of the Mary Stuart story. It began with her life at the French court with Francis II, under the tutelage of Mary of Guise, and introduced Bothwell early in the action as a courier from the Earl of Moray in Scotland, inviting her to return as Queen. When she does she meets with the coolness of the Protestant nobles and the hostility of the fanatical John Knox. The jealousy of Elizabeth is an active force, demonstrated by her dispatch of the weak, effeminate Darnley to scheme on her behalf. Thereafter the other familiar episodes in the drama fall into place: Mary's marriage to Darnley, the murder of Rizzio, her escape with the help of Bothwell from the Scottish nobles, Darnley's murder with Bothwell's assumed incrimination, Mary's abdication, her imprisonment in England and her execution many years later at Fotheringay.

The treatment was written by John Hale and the film was directed by Charles Jarrott. Vanessa Redgrave, whose heroines are never negligible creations, tried to make a positive figure of Mary and gave the film some convincing moments; but the inconsistencies in the Queen's record defeated her, as has so often been the case. Glenda Jackson's Queen Elizabeth was a scheming, suspicious rival, fearing until the end usurpation by Mary. Jarrott's distancing himself from Scotland was reflected in the casting. Most of the players were English, although there were small parts for Tom Fleming and Andrew Keir. The photography was by Christopher Challis, who gave a film shot mainly in the studio some exciting moments of exterior action – figures on horseback in pursuit across landscapes. If the subject of Mary Stuart is attempted again it is more likely to be in terms of Sandy Mackendrick's conception than as a studio-bound costume drama.

The Wicker Man (1973) was a mystery thriller unrelated to any other style of film-making in Scotland. It was set in the Western Isles but there any similarity ended. The story was by Anthony Shaffer, brother of Peter Shaffer of *Equus*, and was rich in eerie invention. On a Hebridean island a twelve-year-old girl has disappeared and a police sergeant is sent to investigate. He is disturbed by what he finds: disregard for Christian doctrine, sexual permissiveness and a denial in the community that the girl ever existed. Her name is in the school register but there is no death certificate and when he investigates further he discovers a dead rabbit in her coffin. Explanations when they come include the reason for the islanders' paganism and the sinister significance of the 'wicker man', a giant sacrificial pyre. Shaffer and the director, Robin Hardy, aided by the camerawork of Harry Waxman and the art direction of Seamus Flannery, relentlessly created an atmosphere of unease, relieved only in the spine-chilling finale, with the half-crazed islanders surrounding the blazing pyre and singing 'Summer is Icumin In'. Edward Woodward, Britt Ekland, Diane Cilento and Christopher

Lee had the main parts and there were contributions by the gifted Scottish comic actor Walter Carr, seldom seen on the cinema screen, and Russell Waters, who is best remembered for his performance in Dr Richard Massingham's *Tell Me If It Hurts*. A contemporary critic found the film 'an immensely enjoyable piece of hokum, thoroughly well researched, performed and directed'.

Like the islands, Scotland's castles had a strong attraction for film-makers. I recall a visit in 1966 by Serge Bourguignon whose *Sundays and Cybèle* won an Oscar for the best foreign language film in 1962. He was looking for a castle as the main location for a film which emerged as *Two Weeks in September*, starring Brigitte Bardot and James Robertson-Justice. In Edinburgh I showed him a compilation film which began in the Borders and covered most of the country. We had reached only Dirleton Castle in East Lothian when he said, 'That's it'. We had lunch in Dirleton at the Open Arms Hotel, well known to *bon vivants*, and I think that clinched it. It became the unit's headquarters. Brigitte Bardot's presence there certainly gave the other guests and staff something to remember. Given its première at the Edinburgh Film Festival in 1967, the film was, however, something to forget. (Perhaps all was not lost. Gunther Sachs, Brigitte's then husband, visited the hotel during the location shooting. I introduced him to my favourite malt whisky, Glenmorangie. When he left he said to the barman, 'I would like thirty-six'. The barman: 'Thirty-six bottles, sir!' 'No, no. Thirty-six cases'.)

Another French director, Bertrand Tavernier, made more rewarding use of Scottish backgrounds for his film *Death Watch* (1980). 'No other city', he said of Glasgow, 'has impressed me so forcefully: a rich nineteenth-century town, now strangely depopulated'. His adapation of David Compton's American novel, *The Continuous Katherine Mortenhoe*, opened with shots of gravestones in Glasgow's Necropolis (a much-filmed setting), the camera rising to reveal a bleak cityscape of dreary tenements and smokestacks under ominous skies. The story is set in some future era when death by disease has become virtually unknown and people die only of old age. A television producer conspires with a doctor who tells a patient she has only three weeks to live and persuades her to be

61. Claire Grogan and Bill Paterson in Bill Forsyth's *Comfort and Joy* (1984):
an unfunny situation, a strangely unresolved plot, and the director's
last film before leaving for the US.

continuously filmed by an employee with a camera implanted in his brain.

A film of both complexity and depth was developed with comprehensive skill by a director of imagination. Its excellencies embraced the camerawork of Pierre-William Glenn, the music of Antoine Duhamel and the acting of Romy Schneider, Harvey Keitel, Harry Dean Stanton and Max von Sydow. A French-West German co-production with international involvement at every level, *Death Watch* stood apart from other film-making in Scotland. The locations in Glasgow and other parts of Scotland were important for the production, but the subject was bigger than its background. If the director was initially attracted by what one critic called 'the picturesque decay' of Glasgow, others today would find decay increasingly difficult to locate in a city which is miles better, both in hype and in reality.

David Puttnam's *Chariots of Fire* (1981) could not have been made but for the life and example of Eric Liddell which gives it a claim to be a Scottish film. Liddell, a young divinity student, stood for qualities which at one time were recognised as identifying characteristics of the Scot: a respect for the Sabbath (even if in Liddell's case it meant the loss of an Olympic medal), missionary zeal, a delight in athleticism, a kind of innocence in a wicked world. In the film Liddell is unmoved by the arguments of the British Olympic administrators: that is his conflict. Harold Abrahams's is different: his conflict is with anti-semitism and racial prejudice. These clashes extend the range of the film but its focus is the Olympic scene itself in Paris in 1924, with its moments of high drama and triumph for the athletes.

Hugh Hudson skilfully manipulated the story to realise maximum suspense and human interest. Ian Charleson was an excellent choice for Liddell, a character combining a simple charm with iron determination. His running action, with head thrown back and arms swinging, made an image which stays in the memory. 'When I run I can feel His pleasure', he said. Ben Cross as Abrahams had the more difficult part, requiring subtlety in conveying the racial element in the theme. It was in evidence most obviously in the confrontation scene at Cambridge University with the masters, played by John

Gielgud and Lindsay Anderson. The slow-motion photography, especially in the training runs on the beach at Gullane, enhanced the visual impact. Iain Smith was responsible for the locations, a service for Puttnam which earned him similar work on *The Killing Fields* and *The Mission*. The film gained much from the plangent music of Vangelis, used at different tempos to great effect throughout.

Chariots of Fire was a well-timed film, arriving when world interest in international sport was in the ascendancy. It won an Oscar for the Best Film in 1981. It may not have staying power but it gave a lot of pleasure in the cinemas and on television. It was a worthy tribute to Eric Liddell, a hero to every Scottish schoolboy in his day.

62. John McGrath's *Blood Red Roses* (1986), the story of a brave and rebellious Sutherland schoolgirl: a courageously unromantic view of Scottish life. Left to right: Gregor Fisher, Elizabeth Maclennan, and Myra McFadyen.

9

Two Bills and Some Others

When Bill Douglas set out to make what he hoped would be a trilogy about his childhood the omens could hardly have been favourable. The setting was Newcraighall, a run-down mining village to the south-east of Edinburgh: typical of many such villages in Scotland, with their back-to-back brick-built houses, bleak surroundings and the refuse bing from the mine just along the road. Inside the houses were equally austere, especially in the period of rationing just after World War II. There was nothing to relieve the gloom, except the director's imagination and the response he could draw from his players. It was a tough way to begin.

Bill Douglas had courage and conviction, qualities which have distinguished all individualists in film-making. Financial help came from the British Film Institute's Production Board, embarking on its first feature film. Douglas had had experience of acting in London as a student with Joan Littlewood and had also had two years at the London Film School. With this minimal schooling he returned to the village where he grew up and began work on *My Childhood* (1972). The leading part was played by Stephen Archibald who, with a fellow pupil, Hugh Resterick, was playing truant on the day Douglas met them in Edinburgh. The others he recruited included several with acting experience, Jean Taylor-Smith, Paul Kermack, Helena Gloag and Eileen McCallum among them.

The trilogy begins in 1945 when there were still German prisoners-of-war working in the fields. The focus for the action was the kitchen of the house where Jamie, the central character, lives with his grandmother and elder brother Tommy. Neither boy is sure of his parentage but Tommy believes that the man who brings him a canary for his birthday is his father. The canary, hidden in the cellar, becomes a symbol of the deprivation suffered by the boys: in the cellar it is eaten by the cat, starved as they are, and the cat is beaten to death. Jamie's only friend is a German prisoner-of-war working on a neighbouring farm and when, at the end of the war, he is sent home, Jamie is distraught. Life becomes even grimmer for him when he is taken by his grandmother to see a woman in a mental home who is revealed as his mother and later, his grandmother, having collapsed in her chair, is feared dead. The first episode (of about fifty minutes' duration) ends with Jamie on the roof of a train, onto which he has jumped from a bridge, pulling away from the village.

My Ain Folk (1973), about the same length, has the two boys alone in the world. Tommy is taken off to a welfare home while Jamie appears to have the better prospect of life with his paternal grandmother. Jamie soon realises, however, that he is unloved and unwanted. He becomes involved – only to be rejected – in a number of personal relationships: with his father who is living next door with another woman; with his grandfather who has just returned from hospital and is having an affair with a woman in the village. There are other complications before the death of his grandfather and Jamie's removal to a welfare home.

In the concluding, longest episode, *My Way Home* (1978), Jamie is withdrawn by his father from the home where he has been sympathetically treated, and returns to Newcraighall. Given his nature and his experiences, he is suspicious of his stepmother and resentful of her son. His paternal grandmother still lives next door where at first he finds some affection, soon to be replaced by hostility. His father tries to send him down the mine. After a series of jobs and nights in Salvation Army hostels, he is conscripted into the Royal Air Force and posted to Egypt. Here he is befriended by a fellow conscript from a different background and is brought into contact for the first time with literature and the arts. He begins to come to terms with himself and to leave behind his self-pitying and dissatisfied adolescence. The trilogy ends with an invitation to visit the home of his new-found friend. There is a final glimpse of the now deserted and dilapidated house at Newcraighall.

I have given the story in some detail as it exposes both its nature and the determination of Bill Douglas not to compromise or soften any of its harshness. This is an unremittingly honest portrayal of a deprived childhood, spent in the bleak setting of a mining village and unrelieved by the affection and understanding of parents and relatives. The director makes no concessions, either in the grim detail of the action or in the sparse dialogue. More words might have made it too easy to sympathise with Jamie. When he has to endure silence and estrangement so also have we. For most of the trilogy, until it reaches its concluding passage, Jamie is an isolated figure, in the earlier episodes at least accepting apathetically the slings and arrows of outrageous fortune. Since this is an autobiographical film, we recognise the accumulation of cruelty and injustice suffered by the growing boy and the size of the effort he makes to survive. Is his fate at least partly self-induced and could he have made more effort to escape? These questions may arise in afterthought but they do not emerge while we are in the grip of the action.

This is a director's, not an actor's, film. Stephen Archibald does convey all that Douglas intends, sometimes by being placed in a lonely setting, sometimes by remaining a silent witness of the domestic upheavals around him. In the first episode there is a performance full of character by Jean Taylor-Smith as the tetchy old grandmother. Paul Kermack played Jamie's father, Karl Fieseler the German prisoner-of-war and Helena Gloag Tommy's mother. Hugh Resterick played Tommy in the first and second episodes. Lennox Milne appeared in the final episode where the part of the youth who begins to transform Jamie's life was well played by Joseph Blatchley. Douglas had a different cameraman in each episode but clearly he was in charge himself of the visual expression of his ideas.

The trilogy won high critical acclaim. Philip French wrote in *The Observer*: 'It is a bleak, almost physically painful picture, distilled from the bitter memories of one of this country's most original talents. I believe this trilogy will come to be regarded not just as a milestone, but as one of the heroic achievements of the British cinema'. Eric Rhode wrote in *The Listener*: 'Genuine film-makers are hard to come by and Douglas, I am convinced, is one of them: he has the ability to describe the most subtle motives and changes of feeling through visual images. He knows how to tell a story in cinematic terms – and he has an extraordinary story to tell'. From

173

the *Los Angeles Times*: 'These first two sections are arguably the finest achievements in the narrative film to arrive from Britain in at least a decade'. The trilogy stood above and apart from any other Scottish film. Only with *The Brave Don't Cry*, by chance a story also drawn from mining, could any acceptable comparison be made.

Bill Douglas went on to make *Comrades* (1987) – with a budget of over £2.25 million, in contrast to the small sums spent on his Scottish films. The story of the Tolpuddle Martyrs, it was shot in Dorset and Australia, which places it outside the subject of this book but not beyond a gesture of recognition towards a film-maker ambitiously extending his range.

Meanwhile another Scottish film-maker with a very different approach was about to emerge. For some fifteen years before *That Sinking Feeling* (1979), Bill Forsyth had been making documentaries, working with one or other of the Scottish companies. He had held in check his ambition to direct feature films but there had been a hint or two of his light touch, notably in *Come Away In*, a film in which he appeared to explain how to run an electricity showroom. This version was declined by its sponsors for not taking the subject sufficiently seriously.

Like Bill Douglas he was also confident and determined. And like Bill Douglas, and any film-maker anywhere, he had first to find the money. He had already written the script for a film which was later to become *Gregory's Girl* and had failed to find sponsorship for it. *That Sinking Feeling* was made, as it were, on the rebound of that rebuff. He was able to raise, from various sources, about £3,000, 'for the things that love and loyalty can't buy', and, of much more importance, to obtain the co-operation of the Glasgow Youth Theatre and a group of technicians who, believing in what he was attempting, worked for nothing. They called themselves the Minor Miracle Film Co-operative. It was a brave gesture and all honour to Bill Forsyth for making it.

That Sinking Feeling was set as firmly in contemporary Glasgow as any of the Ealing comedies were in post-war London as a background. It is about a group of unemployed teenagers who plan what they call 'the perfect crime' – the robbery of a warehouse

63. Giovanni Mauriello and Phyllis Logan in Michael Radford's *Another Time, Another Place* (1983): the timeless quality of an honestly made film.

containing stainless steel sinks. The robbery is successful; but they cannot find a market for their sinks, although one little pile of them is hailed as a masterpiece of avant-garde art by Richard Demarco. The comedy is in the sharply observed detail of life in Glasgow: plans for the robbery are discussed in the rain beneath a statue of Thomas Carlyle, suggestive of Victorian disapproval of such escapades. Perhaps in some sequences the comic momentum is lost; perhaps one or two sequences are held too long; perhaps Forsyth does not quite know how to end his film, well aware that he never intended it to have any message or make any social comment. None of these possible defects diminish the achievement of the film, a joyous and genuine comedy, rooted in everyday urban life and growing out of an affection for the city of Glasgow.

That Sinking Feeling had its première at the Edinburgh Film Festival on August 29, 1979. 'I went into the cinema one kind of person and came out another', said Bill Forsyth in an interview with Liz Taylor. 'I was completely dazed because people kept coming up to me and saying strange things like "You mustn't compromise yourself". It was all surreal, because the night before I had been walking around Edinburgh sticking up posters for the film and now here were the most eminent critics in the film business saying these weird things to me. You are allowed one chance in Scotland', he continued, 'and if you blow it, that's your lot. It is just luck if it comes off. Afterwards, you are terrified, but at the time you don't realise what is happening'.

Bill Forsyth took his success with a likeable modesty. His film was shot in 16mm and subsequently blown up to 35mm for cinema showing. For him it meant that he could raise £250,000, half from Scottish Television and the other half from the National Film Finance Corporation, to make *Gregory's Girl* (1980). Here the setting, essential for the nature of the film, was Cumbernauld near Glasgow, one of Scotland's New Towns. Forsyth himself called it 'a romance about being modern in a New Town environment'. Its central figure is a diffident, gangling teenager with a passion for football and not much success with girls. His is a fantasy life in which he stars, whether he is dodging blows from imaginary opponents or scoring brilliant goals for the school team. But he loses his place in the team to a girl who is a much better player than he is. Again the film is an accumulation of detail. All the characters, teachers and pupils alike, are not quite what they seem. The headmaster plays yesterday's tunes on an old piano during lunchbreak. One pupil is a reporter for the school magazine conducting 'in depth' interviews, another imagines himself to be a pastry cook while a third is a photography nut. There is a clear distinction between the boys, unsophisticated and gullible, the immature voyeurs of the opening shot of a nurse undressing, and the girls, cool and assured, confidently making fun of the trusting Gregory.

With a second film a Bill Forsyth style was becoming apparent: a quirky sense of humour, a preference for amiable eccentricity, a reluctance to identify anything remotely evil in his characters and situations. His unkindest critics were beginning to find his films twee but others (Alan Brien, for example) found 'a cutting edge, an affectionate delicacy, and a free-wheeling impulsive gaiety'. In *Gregory's Girl*, again made with the participation of the Glasgow Youth Theatre, he had two players who responded admirably to this approach: Gordon John Sinclair as the fantasist hero Gregory and Dee Hepburn as the confident heroine. There were also the Scottish comedian Chic Murray as the headmaster, an undemanding part for so talented an actor, and Jake D'Arcy as the games master struggling with his incompetent team.

Bill Forsyth has said, 'I'm really a didactic film-maker and I like a serious message in a film. But I have to put in jokes as that's what audiences like'. It is certainly what audiences came to expect from his films. It may have been a snare from which he had to escape in order to mature as a film director. For better or worse, the whimsical style influenced the work of his contemporaries who were trying to make their way into feature film-making.

Bill Forsyth's next film was *Local Hero* (1983). With David Puttnam of *Chariots of Fire* as producer, a substantial budget (£3 million), a large crew of technicians and Burt Lancaster heading a professional cast, Forsyth moved up several rungs on the international production ladder. Developed from an idea suggested by Puttnam, the film was from Forsyth's own script. In the context of this book his conception of what he hoped to do is important:

I saw it along the lines of a Scottish Beverly Hillbillies – what would happen to a small community when it suddenly became immensely rich – that was the germ of the idea and the story built itself from there. It seemed to contain a similar theme to *Brigadoon*, which also involved some Americans coming to Scotland, becoming part of a small community, being changed by the experience and affecting the place in their own way. I feel close in spirit to the Powell and Pressburger feeling, the idea of trying to present a cosmic viewpoint to people, but through the most ordinary things. And because both this film and *I Know Where I'm Going* are set in Scotland, I've felt from the beginning that we're walking the same . . . treading the same water.

The story concerns the proposal of an oil tycoon in Houston, Texas, to site an oil refinery around a remote West Highland coastal village. He dispatches a junior executive to buy the land. He is met in Aberdeen by the firm's local representative and after briefing at the research laboratories, they set out for the West Coast. In the village the local hotel proprietor is also chartered accountant, game-dealer and accepted by the community as chief negotiator. As the Highland charm works on the American, the negotiations proceed amicably until it is discovered that the rights to the beach belong to an old beachcomber who is determined not to sell them. On the night of a ceilidh, the American is astonished by the appearance of the Northern Lights and, on the telephone to Houston, describes both the Aurora Borealis (the tycoon has an obsession with astrology) and the resistance to the development proposal. The tycoon flies over, is captivated by the Highland way of life and decides to have a marine research institute instead of an oil refinery.

On this bare outline Bill Forsyth builds his film about change. The young executive loses his taste for big business and his boss realises that the preservation of an age-old environment is more important than the making of a temporary fortune. Again the director laces his film with eccentricity and paradox. The local clergyman is a black African educated at a Presbyterian mission, a Russian trawler skipper who comes ashore to attend the ceilidh is a dedicated capitalist and Country-and-Western singer, the oceanographer from

64. Jack Shea and Allen Moore's *The Shepherds of Berneray* (1981): an
admirable documentary, innocent of special pleading or patronising,
springing from an interest in anthropology.

the research laboratory reappears as a mermaid, the canny beach-comber is the very embodiment of contradiction. Add the pursuit of the tycoon by a crazy psychotherapist engaged to divert him from his obsession with the stars and a punk motorcyclist who menaces the young executives whenever they appear in the village street and we have the characteristic elements of a Bill Forsyth film. Burt Lancaster is the Houston tycoon bested by Fulton Mackay's deter-mined beachcomber, Peter Riegert plays the thrusting executive (his 'McIntyre' conceals his Hungarian immigrant parentage) and Peter Capaldi is his Scottish assistant who speaks a dozen languages but has no Gaelic. The photography of Chris Menges (soon to move to directing his own films) succeeds in making the most of the two locations married for the film: the sandy, sun-filled beach at Camusdarach between Arisaig and Mallaig and the delightful Banffshire fishing village of Pennan.

In one of his interviews about the making of *Local Hero* David Puttnam said, 'I quite consciously wanted to make a film where the content swamped the style'. Remove the style from *Local Hero* and the content must seem slender. Bill Forsyth shies away from confrontation with a theme. Despoilation of the West Coast of Scotland through oil exploration and exploitation is a real theme. He chooses to treat it in terms of a self-confessed *Brigadoon* fairy tale. That was his decision and Puttnam must have concurred. Forsyth lives in a gentle, innocent world where there is no evil and very little cynicism. He believes that the world, especially the Scotland he knows and loves, is not such a bad place in which to live and *Local Hero*, like his other films, expresses this affection and devotion. His films seem to echo 'there is Hope', and when so many concentrate on the grim reality of contemporary life that is no bad thing. It is refreshing to find optimism in the work of a young Scottish film-maker.

In *Comfort and Joy* (1984) Bill Forsyth returned to Glasgow, with a story he had written himself. 'When I started out to write it', he said, 'I wanted it to be funny, but I realised it wasn't funny quite early and certainly, when we were filming, I didn't think it was funny at all'. *Comfort and Joy* begins with an unfunny situation. His hero is a disc jockey, on the early morning shift at the local commercial radio station. Between advertisements for sweeties he broadcasts comfort and joy to all his listeners. When he returns to his apartment his unpredictable girlfriend begins to behave oddly, packing belongings away in cardboard boxes. She tells him she is leaving him and within minutes the removal men arrive to strip the place, leaving only the bed, a book and some Christmas lights. He is told by a medical friend that, at thirty-five, he is fortunate in having the opportunity to start again. At the radio station he is obliged to maintain a flow of cheerful chit-chat when he feels no inclination to do so. By chance, in pursuit of another girl, he becomes involved in a territorial war between two ice-cream firms. He becomes a kind of war correspondent for his radio station as the clashes become uglier. As Christmas approaches he realises that changing his life is not going to be easy.

In comments he made at the time, Bill Forsyth seemed to be aware of the narrative problem he created for himself. His disc jockey, so convincingly played by Bill Paterson, is a real character whose discomfiture at the loss of his girlfriend reaches out to the audience. However unhappy he is, he must display undiminished cheerfulness when addressing the microphone. This is a strong human situation which could have made a film on its own. With the introduction of the ice-cream war there is a new situation. The more there is of it the weaker the story line becomes. Forsyth explained that what interested him was the banality of the situation in which the disc jockey found himself. 'His whole life at the radio station is dominated by confectionery; all the ads he does are for sweeties'. When he does try to take himself seriously, against a background of actual warfare and catastrophe, 'he doesn't escape from his own shallow self because the only war that comes to hand is an ice-cream war'.

The two themes do not fuse convincingly. Bill Paterson is a highly intelligent actor, capable of both depth and subtlety in characterisation, and the opening sequences, concerned with loneliness and isolation, are moving. Because they are, involvement in the ice-cream war seems a trivialising irrelevance (even although there was a real conflict in Glasgow at the time of the film's release). The ice-cream war could also have made a film on its own, a low-key echo of what happened in Chicago in the twenties. In defence, Forsyth maintained that 'The whole action of the film takes place in that raw area where nothing could be resolved'. But, ever since the simplicities of the-boy-and-the-girl-and-who-gets-who, the resolution of conflict is what is expected from a film, as from any other form of creative expression. A film should march and build, not dwindle.

Forsyth again had the helpful collaboration of the photographer, Chris Menges. He saw the task as capturing the director's 'genius for elusive comedy' which took 'enormous application to interpret on to the screen'. In his team was Paddy Higson who had been associate producer on *That Sinking Feeling* and *Gregory's Girl*. The producers were Clive Parsons and Davina Belling who had also worked with Forsyth on *Gregory's Girl* and were sympathetic to his style. The players included the versatile Alex Norton, and Rikki Fulton, who had made the most of a very small part in *Local Hero*. Bill Forsyth now had creative collaboration reminiscent of Ealing.

Forsyth left Scotland to make *Housekeeping* (1987) in British Columbia. He took with him his preoccupation with loneliness, his shrewd observation of character and, under restraint, his sense of humour. Victoria Mather wrote in the *Daily Telegraph* that it was 'an intelligent study of the resilience of the young pitted against the transience of adults' affections. *Housekeeping* is full of quirky events and relationships while retaining a detailed grip on reality'. The film reflected a growing confidence in Forsyth's handling of his women characters. Perhaps this burgeoning maturity will be reflected in his next Scottish film. This was scheduled to be *Rebecca's Daughter*, based on a Dylan Thomas screenplay about the Tollgate hooded raiders. He was confident he could find parts of Scotland which would look like Wales.

Meanwhile a third substantial figure was beginning to make a mark, initially through television work in London. Edinburgh-born John Mackenzie began as an assistant to Ken Trodd and gained experience with Ken Loach and Tony Garnett before he directed the film version of John McGrath's play by the 7:84 Company, *The Cheviot, the Stag and the Black, Black Oil* (1974). Covering three

65. Bill Bryden's *Ill Fares The Land* (1982): set on St Kilda but shot in Applecross, the elusive truth lay somewhere else.

centuries, its targets were the Clearances, which in the Highlands made way for sheep, the creation of deer forests for rich sportsmen, and the acquisition in the North Sea of what many regarded as 'Scotland's Oil'. The main argument was that 'until economic power is in the hands of the people their culture will be destroyed' – an argument presented with passion and power. In such a politically oriented production it would have been unreasonable to expect an informed and impartial depiction of the Clearances, always easier to present emotionally than in terms of economic reality. Perhaps some day a film-maker will have the courage to show that emigration from the Highlands was part of an inevitable process as a relief from over-crowding. In the words of Dr T. C. Smout: 'The misery of the Highlands is primarily the misery of the congested, not of the dispossessed'. The exception was, of course, Sutherland where the arch villain was Patrick Sellar who was responsible for the destruction of homes, in one or two cases while old people were still in them. These incidents were unchallengeable and much was made of them. But change there had to be if the people of the Highlands were not to be imprisoned in an unacceptably impoverished way of life. (Something of this broader approach was to be found in Grampian Television's admirable series *The Blood is Strong* (1988) by Ted Brocklebank and Bernd Schulze, which reflected the point of view of the descendants overseas of the nineteenth century emigrants from Scotland.)

In the oil sequence the attitude was overtly anti-American. On the stage, when I first saw it, the play had topicality to increase its impact. In the film there remained old songs and old sorrows and a very strong feeling of exploitation. Interviews filmed in the Highlands and islands lent verisimilitude to the arguments. There were some performances to admire. Bill Paterson had one of his earliest opportunities to show his skill and resource in several parts, including an oil man from Houston. John Bett appeared to relish his portrayal of unpopular characters, and Dolina Maclennan gave emotional power to the songs. A television critic, Nancy Banks Smith of *The Guardian*, wrote of the production that it 'was as slanted as a mountain slope and as exhilarating as ski-ing down it. And with enough faith and malice to move a mountain. I hope'.

Two Bills and Some Others

In *Just Another Saturday* (1975) Mackenzie and Peter McDougall, his scriptwriter, found their theme in the religious tensions in Glasgow and the mood of violence they foster. The central figure was a seventeen-year-old boy, leader of the band in the annual Orange Day Parade. The film followed him through the day, from eager anticipation at the outset through bigotry erupting the carnival atmosphere to violence at the end of it. The boy contemplates the divisions between Catholic and Protestant and tries to come to an understanding of the conflict. John Morrison played the boy and there were parts for Eileen McCallum, Bill Henderson and Ken Hutchinson. The film showed how The Troubles in Northern Ireland are shared to some degree with Glasgow.

Just a Boy's Game (1979), also written by Peter McDougall, was set in Greenock and again had violence as its theme, but without religious involvement. A local hard man is determined to maintain his reputation when challenged by an opposing gang, his motive apparently being to gain the respect of his sour old grandfather, himself a noted exponent of violence. The tenements and dockyards of the shipbuilding port became a battleground, 'a world of cowboy violence in a blighted urban wasteland', in the words of one critic who thought that although the film offered no solutions, 'it underlines the waste and indignity of street brawling'. Perhaps *Dead End Kids* did much the same for an earlier generation.

For their next subject Mackenzie and McDougall chose the life of Jimmy Boyle. Produced by Jeremy Isaacs for Scottish Television, *A Sense of Freedom* (1981) was loosely based on Boyle's autobiography of the same name. The project aroused much opposition in various quarters. Permission to film in Scottish prisons was withheld and Kilmaninham Jail in Dublin was used. There were also problems about shooting in council houses and in a pub, while the Glasgow Fire Brigade was in trouble through providing rain. In their defence the film-makers claimed: 'The film will portray Boyle as he was, a vicious, ruthless thug'. The circumstances which made Boyle into a thug were suggested elliptically. Imprisonment in Barlinnie and the influence of the experimental Special Unit there did change Boyle's life. 'I have caused much suffering and have suffered but the disease is much larger than me', said Boyle. 'An environment

185

has been created that has encouraged change and I'm the vehicle that the lesson is travelling in'. When a retrospective of his films was included in the programme of the 1980 Edinburgh Film Festival, the director's treatment of a difficult subject was regarded as 'a decided move away from naturalism, towards a carefully constructed theatricality which Mackenzie felt was the most fitting form for the expression of Boyle's inner development'. The uncompromising work of Mackenzie and McDougall could be regarded as a corrective for the escapist element in Scottish cinema. Either element alone could not be held to give a balanced picture of the country.

David Hayman's performance as Boyle was highly praised, 'mesmerising from the first swagger to the ambivalent fade-out'. In the large cast there were parts for the versatile Alex Norton, Jake D'Arcy and Fulton Mackay, in one of his inflexible police inspector roles.

Blood Red Roses (1986) was a film version of a play by John McGrath first presented by his 7:84 Theatre Company. It was the story of a Sutherland schoolgirl of rebellious temperament who greets her father, whom she has never seen, when he returns from the Korean war with one leg blown away. Her mother departs and she and her father move to Glasgow, her spirit at least undefeated. As she grows into womanhood she fights all the way, against social injustice, class discrimination and deprivation of all kinds. In her employment she is militant, a leader of revolt against working conditions; and when her marriage fails she is driven to the edge of defeat – but not over. McGrath presented his case history with power and conviction and made clear where his sympathies lay. He had the co-operation of an experienced cast, led by Elizabeth Maclennan as the adult rebel. James Grant was the disabled father and Gregor Fisher, an often under-rated Scottish actor, the workmate who marries her. John McGrath's film joined the work of John Mackenzie and Bill Douglas in presenting a courageously unromantic view of Scottish life.

Another director, an early graduate from the National Film and Television School, who was to make a significant contribution to

66. Murray Grigor's *Scotch Myths* (1982): Samuel Fuller (right) returns to Scotland to direct a mocked-up Brigadoon II. For Scots it seemed a waste of resources to perpetuate the tartan preoccupation in this way: a puzzling contribution to national projection.

Scottish cinema had emerged at the same time as John Mackenzie. Michael Radford had given a hint of his quality in *The Last Stronghold of the Pure Gospel* (1979), a record of a community on the island of Lewis in the Outer Hebrides committed to the ideal of pure Calvinism, living under the threat of hellfire and damnation. Its authenticity as a document was never in question. The psalms in Gaelic added to the sense of another world.

Radford followed this with *The White Bird Passes* (1980), also produced for BBC Scotland. The first part of the film was adapted from the autobiographical novel by Jessie Kesson, well-known for her down-to-earth stories of North-east Scotland. It concerned the relationship between a nine-year-old girl and her prostitute mother and their years of poverty in Elgin. The second part was a contemporary documentary about Jessie herself, talking about how she gave fictional form to her experiences and overcame adverse circumstances. The whole film was alight with the burning sincerity of a remarkable woman.

Radford's association with Jessie Kesson, and with Phyllis Logan who appeared in *The White Bird Passes*, continued and flourished in *Another Time, Another Place* (1983). Adapted from a short novel by Kesson, it was set in the Black Isle, the fertile peninsula (not an island) between the Firths of Beauly and Cromarty. One of its many virtues was the sensitive rendering of the countryside and the farming year: the low hills rising from the waterside; the sowing of the grain, its ripening, harvesting and the threshing in the farmyard, dominated by the noisy, smoky steam engine; the potato planting in the precisely turned furrows; the singling and eventual picking of the turnips; a midnight calving at the farm. All of this activity, so distinctive a part of the Scottish farming scene and here essential to the development of the story, was photographed over the changing seasons with great skill by Roger Deakins so that the film, if incidentally, was a unique record, as faithful and comprehensive as any documentary. 'Nothing chocolate boxy about the landscape', said Jessie Kesson. 'Beautiful, yes, but also harsh and unsparing'.

Into this setting comes an army lorry with Italian prisoners-of-war to work on the land. Three of them are allocated to a farm in the small community and are billeted in a bothy across the yard from the farmhouse. The farmer is a dour, unresponsive character. His childless wife, fifteen years younger, feels straitened by her unsatisfactory marriage and the dull, demanding routine of her life. The three Italians, in their different ways, suggest a more alluring world than anything she has experienced. One is a teacher from Tuscany, another a carpenter from Rome and the third, Luigi, an exuberant barrow boy from Naples. She shows them how to control a Tilley lamp, perhaps a reflection of what is happening to her, and sympathises with Luigi who is disconsolate about the rainy weather and 'nothing for look'. At first she resists his advances and his blunt pleas for 'jiggy-jig' but gradually her sympathy for his isolation and the sexual neglect of her husband merge in her seduction. She is assailed by guilt but still feels the compulsion of mutual attraction and mutual need.

Michael Radford handled every aspect of the theme with understanding and consummate skill. The Italians with their natural exuberance feel lost in a landscape so often cold and forbidding. The farm workers, who include a woman whose husband has been posted missing at Monte Cassino, find themselves figures of fun, given to antics in the potato fields. Radford carefully sustained this conflict of nationalities, respecting the attitude both of the incomers and the community in which they find themselves. He remained faithful to Jessie Kesson's story, written out of first-hand experience. He also drew from his players exceptionally sensitive performances. Phyllis Logan conveyed the gradual awakening of the young wife, responding to the pushy Neapolitan amorist (Giovanni Mauriello) and guiltily relishing the fruits of passion. Tom Watson's taciturn and unattractive husband was a necessary part of the human equation, while the effervescent Gregor Fisher as master of ceremonies made the lively barn dance as authentic as anything in the film. *Another Time, Another Place* had the timeless quality of an honestly made film.

Another film of conspicuous honesty was *The Shepherds of Berneray* (1981). Berneray is a small island in the Outer Hebrides with a population of just over a hundred, working on crofts and with sheep on land rented from the laird. Through the eyes of a bachelor shepherd and three generations of another family was told the story of a year, encompassing the life of the sheep and showing reactions of crofters and animals to the changing seasons. Underlying this story was the sense of a community in transition, struggling to maintain its Gaelic heritage.

The film stood apart from other production initiatives in Scotland in that it sprang from an interest in anthropology. It was made by Jack Shea and Allen Moore, graduates of Harvard University, who spent about a year on Berneray and shot about fifteen hours of film, edited at Harvard to about an hour. Finance came from the Film Study Center at Harvard, the Highlands and Islands Development Board and the Scottish Arts Council. It was an admirable documentary, innocent of special pleading or patronising: a quietly persuasive account of a way of life, protecting itself from takeover by urban influence.

Gaelic also formed part of the theme of *Hallaig: The Poetry and Landscape of Sorley MacLean* (1984), the Gaelic poet born on the island of Raasay, off Skye. This was a film of quality, fully worthy of its subject. An hour long production from the Island House Workshop, it was satisfying as a biography, with the poet telling much of the story himself. He spoke direct to the camera and, held by his magnetic eyes and his slow, sonorous voice, we came to know the man and gained a fuller understanding of his poetry. McLean's poetry expresses the underlying sadness of the Gael, springing from his exile and exploitation – the 'hardship, wrong, tyranny, misfortune' instanced in his epic poem, 'The Cuillin'. The film too reflected a deep and intense feeling for place. The poet sees not menace in the stark, jagged Cuillins but something heroic. Mark Littlewood, the cameraman, caught superbly the many moods of the Highland landscape – now a soft merging in mist of land and sea, now a fierce piling of ominous cloud on mountain top, now an unbelievable commingling of deepest blue and sunset red. Timothy Neat was the director and the commentary by Iain Crichton Smith, spare and lucid, added to the film's texture.

Timothy Neat and Mark Littlewood collaborated again, with Barbara Grigor as producer, in making *Tree of Liberty* (1987). This was a tribute to the work of the American composer, Serge Hovey, in rewriting the songs of Robert Burns with their original tunes and

67. John Gordon Sinclair in *The Girl in the Picture* (1986) from the second wave of new Scottish films. He appeared first in *Gregory's Girl*.

his own music as accompaniment. The songs were sung by Jean Redpath: they could not have had more sensitive rendering. The film also traced Hovey's heroic effort to cope with the paralysing effect of amyotrophic lateral sclerosis which left him dependent on a breathing machine. Disparate elements were satisfyingly brought together.

A feature film in Gaelic with sub-titles in English, a story set in the sixth century, enacted by unemployed youngsters from Glasgow: a unique combination. Barney Platts-Mills, talented director of *Private Road* and *Bronco Bullfrog*, suddenly decided to leave London and live in a deprived area of Glasgow. While writing a novel and an opera, he came to know the youngsters who hung about the mean streets. He had read J. F. Campbell's *Tales of the Western Highlands* and, on a sudden impulse, decided to make a film of the legend of Finn McCool and the gangs which once roamed the Highlands. Over a period of two years *Hero* (1982) was shot in Argyll while the young players were learning to speak Gaelic. Derek McGuire played the prince sent to join the fabled hero Finn (Alastair Kenneil) only to be seduced by Finn's enchantress-wife (Caroline Kenneil). The acting varied widely. Of more importance was the film's success in conveying a sense of cultural deprivation, an exploited land and a troubled and dispossessed people. Produced by Maya Films for Channel 4, this extraordinary film, the product of a social gesture, was well received by Italian critics at the Venice Film Festival.

Scotland provided backgrounds for parts of a number of films which only in a rather limited sense could be described as Scottish. For example, *Journey to the Centre of the Earth* (1959), an adaptation of the Jules Verne novel, began (and ended) in Edinburgh, with James Mason as a celebrated geologist setting out with a protégé student for Iceland and a descent into the crater of a volcano. Charles Brackett adapted the story and an ingenious piece of science-fiction was directed by Henry Levin.

One of the most spectacular of these quasi-Scottish films was *Highlander* (1986), a wildly fantastic tale which began with a sword fight in the garage of Madison Square Garden and jumped to a medieval battle between the clans in sixteenth century Scotland. It was remarkable for Gerry Fisher's visually exciting photography of

Glen Nevis, Glenfinnan and Eilan Donan and for the performance of Sean Connery. The Edinburgh-born actor has probably appeared in more films than any other Scot but only in *Sean Connery's Edinburgh* has he shown real affinity with his native country. His was a wider world stage but he has made helpful gestures to Scotland through the Edinburgh-based Scottish International Educational Trust, financed by his Bond films.

Bill Forsyth's closest associate, when they made documentaries for Films of Scotland, was Charlie Gormley. Like other contemporaries he was eager to make feature films – 'there was nowhere else to go'. He had had experience in The Netherlands and working for the Children's Film Foundation and knew how to handle actors and dialogue. He is also a writer and wrote the screenplay for *Living Apart Together* (1983), produced for Channel 4 on a budget of £350,000.

Living Apart Together was about a rock-and-roll singer and songwriter who returns to his native city, Glasgow, for the funeral of an old friend. Through discos, bars and the occasional mean street he pursues his errant wife who leaves him for another musician. At the heart of the film was the performance of B. A. Robertson, the Scottish singer and songwriter, playing in effect himself – a devil-may-care big spender. Gormley gave it some neat touches, as in the scene where the hero, interviewed in a bar and unaware that the tape recorder is running, reveals more about his personal life than he intended. The writer/director also gave the film dialogue which rang true. David Anderson played the friend who has remained in Glasgow and is jealous of the hero's success, Barbara Kellerman was the discontented wife and Peter Capaldi the other musician.

Gormley apart, the star of the film was the cameraman, Mark Littlewood, whose photography reminded one critic of *Elvira Madigan*, than which there could be no higher praise. He is one of the technicians whose work has enriched Scottish films over a long period.

Charlie Gormley extended his range with his next film, *Heavenly Pursuits* (1986), again made from his own screenplay. The setting was the Blessed Edith Semple Catholic School in Glasgow where the authorities are looking for miracles which will raise the Blessed Edith to sainthood. This brings them into conflict with one of the teachers who believes that the minor miracles he achieves with his pupils are the only ones of real importance. When he himself begins to be the subject of strange happenings – an escape from injury, extraordinary advances made by previously slow children, and so on – the confidence of the devout music teacher with whom he is in love is shaken.

Gormley's serious treatment of the theme was the source of much of the film's comedy. His writing neatly fitted the characters and gave the situations just enough bite. He had the invaluable assistance of two gifted players: Tom Conti as the teacher who has miraculous powers thrust upon him and Helen Mirren, subtly underplaying as the music teacher. These performances, especially Conti's, gave the film its tone. B. A. Robertson provided the music and the sensitive photography was by Michael Coulter. An adult film which was warmly welcomed when it was shown at the Edinburgh Film Festival in 1986.

It was inevitable that more Scottish film-makers should follow in the whimsical footsteps of Bill Forsyth: if whimsy was what the audiences wanted from Scottish films that is what they would have. When Lloyd's Bank held a national screenplay competition in 1984, it was won by Ninian Dunnett with *Restless Natives* (1985), a comedy about two Edinburgh youths who became Highland highwaymen and, hidden behind carnival masks from a joke shop, hold up coachloads of American tourists, fleece them of their valuables and disappear into the hills. The film had some delightful moments of comic invention and made enterprising use of the Highland landscape. The policemen were pawky and the Americans dim. The youths were played by Joe Mullany and Vincent Friel who had graduated, one from the Glasgow Youth Theatre and the other from Edinburgh's Traverse Theatre. Produced by the Oxford Film Company and given its première at the Warner, Leicester Square, in London, the film was received with tolerance as a product of youthful enterprise in a hard world, although Iain Johnstone in the *Sunday Times* protested that it was old-fashioned and lacking in 'abrasive humour, social statement and, yes, sheer vulgarity'.

194

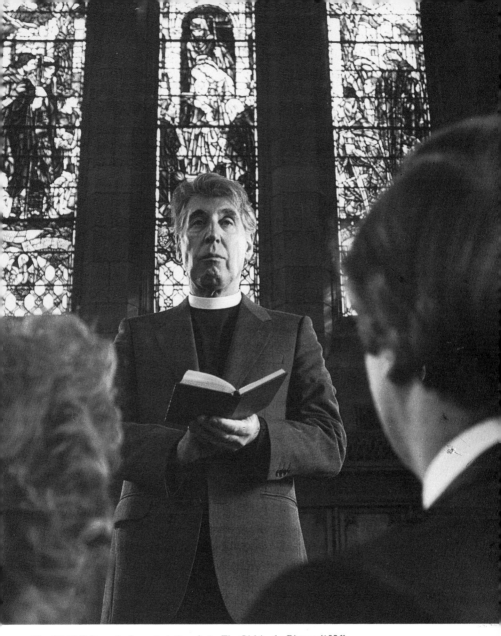

68. Rikki Fulton: A characteristic role in *The Girl in the Picture* (1986).

Associate producer on *Restless Natives* was Paddy Higson who had also been involved in the making of films with Murray Grigor, Bill Forsyth and Charlie Gormley. The first film from her own company, Antonine Productions, was *The Girl in the Picture* (1986), directed by the American, Cary Parker, who also wrote the story. The setting is a photographic agency in Glasgow where a young photographer is trying to generate enough courage to end his relationship with his art student girlfriend. He accepts advice from his assistant, who keeps falling in love with the girls whose photographs he develops. A third young man is about to be married and his eventual wedding forms the centre piece of the film and the inter-relationships, which have become complicated, are resolved.

The film was heavily dependent on performance and personalities. The troubled young photographer was played by Gordon John Sinclair, a slightly older but just as diffident and confused Gregory, while the girl was the delectable Irina Brook. David McKay was the backward lover and his employer, amused by all the immature talk of girl problems, was Paul Young. Gregor Fisher, an actor with a much larger range than he is normally given an opportunity to demonstrate, played the bridegroom whose stag-party is barely over before he is due at the kirk. As Rikki Fulton was the officiating clergyman, the fun in the encounter was brimming over. This may not be the most perceptive treatment of puppy love ever made, but in the short term it was engaging enough and sustained a note of gentle humour.

It was still a very limited picture of Scotland which was emerging from these films. There was life beyond Glasgow. When the film-makers did move outside their choice of subject seemed puzzling. Why did the highly talented stage producer Bill Bryden of the Royal Lyceum Company and the National Theatre, turn to the evacuation of St Kilda as a theme in 1982, more than fifty years after the islanders had left and when there was very little connection between their situation and anything in contemporary Scotland? When Michael Powell made *The Edge of the World* in 1936, the evacuation in 1930 was still comparatively fresh in the public mind; and in 1967 Christopher Mylne had made a record of the bird life of the island group, the awesome precipitous cliffs and the remnants of habitation which, partly because of a month of exceptional sunshine, will never be bettered. Surely Bill Bryden did not agree with the verdict that his *Ill Fares the Land* (1982) was 'the most moving and resonant of all new Scottish films, in which a half-forgotten episode in Scotland's past becomes a powerful and damning allegory of the country's present'? I have seen life at first hand on Foula where Powell made *The Edge of the World*. As a journalist I clearly recall the circumstances of the evacuation of St Kilda where a reasonable twentieth-century life was no longer possible. I have spoken in Melbourne with descendants of the islanders who left Scotland for a happier existence. These experiences do not for me add up to any kind of justification for a film regretting the evacuation. 'I suppose I'm writing about what every scientist calls progress and every artist calls tragedy', said Bryden. The elusive truth lay somewhere else.

Ill Fares the Land was shot at Applecross on the mainland and for anyone who knows village bay on Hirta, the main island in the group, it was difficult to accept the very different landscape. The theme was inevitably the same as Michael Powell's in *The Edge of the World*: the conflict between the older islanders determined to stay and the younger generation anxious to leave. The film tells the story of the last two years, 1928-30, when the conflict is intensifying. The narrator is a young islander who is responsive to the pull of the mainland and whose father, who feels Glasgow is no attraction and who doesn't like the idea of wages, is convinced that the islanders can continue to live as they have always done, with the seabirds providing food and oil and the sheep a meagre income. Ailments such as the influenza germ brought by tourists cause epidemics and reduce the population to a point where evacuation becomes inevitable. A nurse sent by the Scottish Office finally convinces the islanders.

Considerable effort was made to simulate the St Kilda background. A film made on the island group in 1923 by a Glasgow company, Topical Productions, had been studied and the costumes, especially the tammies worn by the men, were carefully reproduced. So also were the groupings of the island parliament – the elders sitting on a row of benches in front of the single storey houses.

George MacInnes played the young islander and James Grant his father and there were confident performances by Fulton Mackay, Robert Stephens, James Copeland and the veteran actress Jean Taylor-Smith to strengthen the human side of the film. I hope Bill Bryden will make more films in Scotland. When he does he may find another theme more relevant to contemporary life in which he can be involved.

I have described how Alexander Korda told the story of Prince Charles Edward Stuart. In *Culloden* (1964) Peter Watkins used it to continue the anti-war campaign he had begun in *The War Game*. On Culloden Moor on April 16, 1746, the Prince's Highland clans face the Duke of Cumberland's army containing some Lowland Scots. Before the battle soldiers in both armies are interviewed and a neutral observer explains troop positions. Cumberland's canonfire decimates the Highlanders and the battle is lost, the film suggests, by indecision on the part of the command. Cumberland enters Inverness in triumph while his troops are ordered to hunt out and kill the Jacobite survivors. This is a prelude to a brief account of the Clearances – enforced migration to make way for sheep.

Among the advisers on the film was Iain Cameron Taylor of the National Trust for Scotland and John Prebble, author of books on Culloden and the Clearances. Watkins had the active collaboration of men, women and children from Inverness. By using a hand-held camera, rapid panning and sudden close-ups he gave the battle scenes an immediacy of impact. There was never any doubt about his sincerity and eagerness to demonstrate the folly of war and its tragic consequences. For many audiences it would be seen as a powerful anti-war document. For Scots it was something more emotionally compelling – the end of a struggle against the English, no matter how little that accorded with the facts. Tears flowed whenever and wherever the film was shown in Scotland.

Fall from Grace (1984) continued the Prince Charlie story after Culloden. In this short film Ian Wyse, a Glasgow graduate from the National Film and Television School, saw the Prince as a hunted figure, moving from cave to cave, in the company of a small group of loyal clansmen: dishevelled, hungry, suffering from dysentry and, in his weariness, making homosexual advances.

69. Sean Connery, born in Edinburgh in 1930, has appeared in scores of films, seven of them as Ian Fleming's James Bond, and is now a force in world film-making. He has still to find a major role in a Scottish production although he made a gesture to his native country in *Sean Connery's Edinburgh*. In *Highlander*, a fantastic tale set partly in Scotland, he appeared as Ramirez, 'a two thousand year old Egyptian-Spanish immortal' (1986).

Dignity has not altogether departed and his followers, who speak in Gaelic among themselves, still address him as Your Highness. All except McGregor, who cannot forget the fate of his family and the hardships imposed on the clans after Culloden. Wyse showed his resources as a director and the power of the medium to lend a deeper meaning to surface action, particularly in the climactic scene where the fugitives celebrate the sighting of the French rescue vessels while the Hanoverian troops are advancing. A dramatic last shot had the Prince, in a white cloak, striding across the moor towards the ships.

The short stories of George Mackay Brown attracted many film-makers to Orkney. They came mainly from television and it becomes ever more difficult to separate work for the two media. *The Privilege* (1983) was, however, made primarily for the cinema. Its director was Ian Knox who studied at the Edinburgh College of Art, spent some time working in film studios in Budapest and eventually returned to Britain to complete his training at the National Film School. *The Privilege* was about *droit de seigneur* in a bucolic setting: a contrast between pre-nuptial celebration with a fiddler leading the wedding procession over the hills to singing and dancing in the barn and the laird's elegant residence with his servant laying down fresh bed-linen. As with so many of Mackay Brown's stories, it was a small segment of Orkney life, sensitively recorded in words and responsively recreated in pictures. His work does not readily lend itself to full-length treatment. Ironically, as I write, his home town of Stromness is providing the background for *Venus Peter*, a feature film from a screenplay by Ian Sellar and Christopher Rush. *The Privilege* was produced by Andrena Finlay and the actors included Brian Cox, James Copeland and Ian Stewart.

With Jenny Brown far away in the Arctic, other film-makers, also by chance women, found subjects in Shetland. *The Work They Say Is Mine* (1986) was directed from her own script by Rosie Gibson, produced by Penny Thomson, photographed by Diane Tammes and edited by Fiona Macdonald. Its theme was the contribution made by women to the economy and life of Shetland, mainly through knitting, crofting and fishing. The manual dexterity of the Shetland women was demonstrated in the intricate patterns of their knitwear, the very soft wool plucked from the island sheep; and in the astonishing speed and skill displayed in the gutting of the herring. Archive material was part of the film's texture.

Several of the shorter films made over this period reflected the input of writer or director. Douglas Eadie, writer of several documentaries and self-appointed outspoken critic of what he called the Scottish film establishment, worked with Brian Crumlish on two films with a literary reference. *The Caledonian Account* (1975) had Thomas Telford, who built the Caledonian Canal in 1803-22, sailing through the waterway in the company of his contemporary, Sir Walter Scott. They spoke about the Highlands, past and present, and the conflict they identified between romance and progress. It was a good idea and the liveliness it engendered was, as Eadie, here the writer, claimed, in contrast to the flatness of many travelogues.

The Garden Beyond (1977) was at once a much more ambitious and a much more difficult film. Its subject was William Soutar, a Scottish poet of the thirties, who, with Hugh McDiarmid, used Scots as distinct from English to express nationalist political themes. He suffered from a spinal disease which made him bedridden for the last thirteen years of his life in his parents' home in Perth. Instead of languishing, his urge to write poetry flourished. Although all he saw of the outer world was the view from his bedroom window, his vision was not cramped. Instead his poetry was intensified in feeling. The film was difficult because the action was confined to the one small setting; but the flow of visitors to the poet's bedside gave it variety. Bertie Scott made Soutar a quietly convincing figure. The success of the film, however, lay in Douglas Eadie's writing, based on Soutar's diaries, and in the unobtrusive direction of Brian Crumlish.

Michael Alexander wrote and directed several films about life on the island of Arran where he was born. *Home and Away* (1974) was about a small boy who leaves Arran to board at a bleak school on the neighbouring island of Bute. In addition to loneliness he has troubles with his schoolmaster while in the background is his knowledge of marital disputation at home. Bill Douglas had a hand in the script and the photography was by Mark Littlewood. *The Tent* (1975) was made on location on Arran and described the differing reactions of a farmer and his adolescent son to a young couple on their land.

Later Alexander and Littlewood made a number of films on subjects drawn from sport, not necessarily Scottish. *No Easy Way* had its climax at the Moscow Olympic Games of 1980, where Allan Wells won his gold and silver medals. *Only a Game* was a series of five fifty-minute documentaries telling the story of Scottish football from the turn of the century until the present day. *Doing the Business* (1988) was about Stephen Hendry, the young snooker champion from Edinburgh.

Douglas Eadie with his co-workers, Michael Alexander and Mark Littlewood, looked beyond Scotland for the theme of their longest and most ambitious literary-political film, *Gramsci* (1987), commissioned by Channel 4 to commemorate the fiftieth anniversary of the death of Antonio Gramsci in Italian fascist captivity. The film showed growing confidence in assembling an argument, drawing as it did on interviews with ex-prisoners who knew Gramsci as well as using archive material and dramatised scenes.

Although the main work of Norman McLaren, the animation artist who began making films at the Glasgow School of Art was done for the National Film Board of Canada, he did produce while at the GPO Film Unit a short Scottish cartoon, *Mony a Pickle* (1938). In the tradition he founded several Scottish artists produced animated films of merit. Donald Holwell made *Sisyphus* (1971) with Robert Garioch reading his own poem. He also drew the animated sequences for Murray Grigor's *Clydescope*. Lesley Keen paid imaginative homage to Paul Klee in *Taking a Line for a Walk* (1983). The art schools in both Edinburgh and Glasgow were fertile fields for film-makers.

Murray Grigor, one of the most talented and unpredictable of Scotland's film directors, had been using his skills in a number of ways. His association with Billy Connolly, begun in his Films of Scotland production *Clydescope*, was continued in *Big Banana Feet* (1976), a record of a tour the comedian made in Ireland. On and off the stage, it delivered the Connolly persona at full strength – the only course to take. It did say something indirectly about Glasgow's verve and vivacity and the record showed that the

70. *Venus Peter* (1989): Gordon R. Strachan as Peter on his grandfather's fishing boat Venus.

audiences loved it. Collaborating with Murray Grigor in writing, production and direction was Patrick Higson, while David Peat and Mark Littlewood were responsible for the photography.

An assignment to make yet another film about Edinburgh was in a sense more demanding: it had all be said and shown before. Yet the outcome, *Sean Connery's Edinburgh* (1982), was highly inventive and original. Grigor had the experienced co-operation of the actor, who had come to know the city of his birth as a delivery boy on a horse-drawn milk float. He responded so well to direction that the film always had a warm, human quality. Connery playing golf in Parliament Square, leaning out of a window in the house where Alexander Graham Bell invented the telephone, or joining a television commentator for a moment of victory at Murrayfield: these were an essential part of the film's fabric. Perhaps its most memorable sequence was set in the picture gallery at the Palace of Holyroodhouse where Grigor filmed the portraits of the kings – and a queen – of Scotland, all painted by the Dutch artist de Witt in his own likeness. Bert Haanstra had used something of the same idea in his *Rembrandt*. Here there was wit as well as ingenuity. The camera (Mark Littlewood) ranged freely over the city, now taking to the air to show the pattern of the New Town's crescents and squares, now exploring the dungeons of Edinburgh Castle with the names of the French prisoners from the Napoleonic War scratched on their doors. It showed how Edinburgh combines the classical and the romantic and its range included Scott, Stevenson and Burns, the traditions of law and medicine, the Botanical Gardens and Arthur's Seat, the Festival and the Tattoo. The credits included Lynda Myles as producer. As writer and director, Murray Grigor's unmistakable stamp was on the film.

Murray Grigor continued to make his architectural films which had made his name known beyond Scotland. The most ambitious was *The Architecture of Frank Lloyd Wright* (1983) for which he spent some time in the United States, on sponsorship from the Arts Council of Great Britain. Again he had David Peat as cameraman, with Michael Coulter.

There was little evidence of the high intelligence and artistic integrity which distinguished Grigor's earlier films in *Scotch Myths*

(1982). This had its origin in the exhibition of the same title which he and Barbara Grigor staged first at St Andrews and later at the 1981 Edinburgh Festival. The idea was apparently sparked off by Grigor's discovery in the United States that Californian orange growers, descendants of Scottish immigrants, were still decorating their crates with pictures of Highland lassies and stags at bay. To this they added examples of other Scottish products – whisky, shortbread, oatcakes, haggis, marmalade – all decked out in tartan and including pictures of Scott, Burns, Bonnie Prince Charlie, Harry Lauder, even Queen Victoria. As an exhibition it was a popular success.

As a film it worked only at moments. One was a sequence set on the island of Staffa at Fingal's Cave where a kind of Liberace figure belted out Mendelssohn's Hebridean music on a white grand piano set in the rocks with the tide steadily rising. Others were the contributions made by John Bett as Byron and McGonagall and the appearance of Bill Paterson as Harry Lauder, marvellously faithful even if a caricature. Much less successful were the interjections of Sam Fuller as a Californian film-maker looking for Brigadoon.

There can be no argument about the abuse of Scottish emblems in portraying Scotland or about the use of the heather and haggis image for commercial purposes. To make a film on this theme, however, is not going to improve the situation. For Scots it seemed a waste of resources to perpetuate the tartan preoccupation in this way. For audiences elsewhere, who might have been interested in an explanation of how these phenomena came about, it must have seemed a puzzling contribution to national projection. For Paul Scott, of the Saltire Society and a diplomat with much overseas service, it was 'an irresponsible and self-indulgent concoction of over-simplification, misrepresentation and malice. It was a series of leaps from unsubstantiated premise to untenable conclusion, without even the saving graces of wit, humour or technical competence'. With Scots, he added 'it must tend to deepen the present mood of weak national self-confidence. With others it can only expose us to ridicule and contempt'. Perhaps that was to take the film too seriously. Certainly there was no doubt about its technical competence. Otherwise I share his estimation of the film.

With *Scotch Myths* out of his system, Murray Grigor, joined by his wife Barbara as producer, could turn to more rewarding subjects. *E. P. Sculptor* (1987) was a film about the work of Eduardo Paolozzi, one of the Italians who have contributed valuably to Scottish cultural life. The artist's concern with the inter-relationship between twentieth century man and industrial technology was explored with sympathetic skill. There were comments from artists and others, including the science fiction writer J. G. Ballard, who suggested that if the twentieth century were lost to history it could be reconstructed in its essentials from Paolozzi's work.

The ever-effervescent Richard Demarco was a natural subject for a director not lacking in effervescence himself. As he had done some twenty years before in Eddie McConnell's film, *Walkabout Edinburgh*, the artist appeared in *The Demarco Dimension – Art in a Cold Climate* (1988) as full of enthusiasm as ever, although here he was concerned not so much with the city of Edinburgh as with his own art gallery and his involvement in the Traverse Theatre, for long the focus for experimental play-writing in the city. It is impossible for Demarco to be still for very long: physically and in conversation he is forever dashing around, always stimulating, often provocative, sometimes penetrating. To be in his company is to feel an irrepressible urge to be up and doing, even if we are sometimes uncertain what to do. He knows what he wants, more money for the arts in Scotland, more awareness of the enrichment art can bring to life. If that often means his own enterprises they have earned such recognition.

Murray Grigor's method was to involve as many people as possible from the wider art world, each making a comment on the Demarco dimension. Ian Barr, a patron of the arts while chairman of the Scottish Postal Board, said it was better to try and fail than not to try at all. Timothy Clifford, Director of the National Galleries of Scotland, thought that if Demarco didn't exist it would have been necessary for Edinburgh to invent him. Jimmy Boyle, the Barlinnie prisoner turned artist, spoke of him as a whirlwind: 'He makes everybody seem special'. Jim Haynes of the Traverse Theatre referred to their early collaboration there and the good that had come from it. The critic Cordelia Oliver spoke knowledgeably

71. The author and film-making friends on the occasion of his retirement in 1975 from Films of Scotland. Left to right: Bill Forsyth, Murray Grigor, Laurence Henson, Mike Alexander, Eddie McConnell, Forsyth Hardy, Mark Littlewood, Patrick Higson, (front) Charlie Gormley, Oscar Marzaroli.

(Photograph, Martin Singleton)

about the experimental art he had brought to Edinburgh, comments which were supported by John Bellany and Sandy Moffat. They paid tribute to his championing of Joseph Beuys at a time when it was not fashionable to do so. These were only a few of the people who spoke warmly about Demarco and his work.

The quick-fire tempo of the film slackened for a few minutes so that Grigor could incorporate the sequence from Bill Forsyth's *That Sinking Feeling* in which Demarco, finding some propped up metal sinks in a warehouse, enthused about them as a marvellous example of modern sculpture. There was a glimpse of Sean Connery before the film ended with a sequence on Demarco's audacious gesture to the 1988 Edinburgh Festival: his production of a version of *Macbeth* on the island of Inchcolm in the middle of the Firth of Forth. No-one but Demarco would have made such a proposal. No-one but Ricky could have realised it, even if the wind and the rain invited pneumonia for those brave enough to make the crossing.

Demarco's work has had recognition: the Italian Honour of Cavaliere Nell 'Ordine Al Merito for his contribution to artistic achievement outside Italy and from H. M. Queen Elizabeth the award of the O. B. E. Gratifying, but what he would like to see is the adequate financing of his art gallery and theatrical enterprise.

Murray Grigor has an ambition, unrealised as I write, to make a film about R. B. Cunninghame Graham, Scottish Nationalist, one time gaucho, explorer, wit, critic, writer and Member of Parliament who rode down Whitehall to Westminster on a white horse. There's a subject to stretch the director of *Mackintosh*! What a splendid addition it would be to his film gallery! How much Scottish cinema would gain from such an international subject!

10

A Will to the Future

There are three essential prerequisites for the making of a film: money, an idea and artists to give it form. This is true of any film made anywhere, and Scotland is no different. The requirements are, of course, interconnected. A money source must be persuaded that the idea will make a film which audiences will wish to pay to see and that the film-makers have the skill and imagination to bring it successfully to the screen.

To achieve that kind of interconnection in Scotland is difficult. Scotland is a small country, however much its influence has spread abroad. United with England and lacking an administration with control of the country's finances, it is unable to provide money from central sources to pay for films. The British Film Institute can meet the cost of such films as the Bill Douglas trilogy. The Scottish Film Council now has a Production Fund with a full-time director, Penny Thomson, whose aim is to provide financial assistance for projects which it believes will contribute to the growth of a national cinema. It has helped to finance a number of short films and, substantially, with the cost of *Venus Peter*. Scottish Television and Channel 4 have both helped with the financing of Scottish films. Money can be lent by the National Film Finance Corporation. These don't provide a very solid basis for continuous feature film-making. So how are Scottish feature films to be financed?

The achievement of Bill Forsyth is one possible answer. Here was a film-maker with determination and initiative. He had many allies when he made *That Sinking Feeling*. To obtain some finance he did not scorn small contributions, from whatever source. By using the Glasgow Youth Theatre he avoided large salary costs for his players. By shooting on 16mm he had minimum outlays on film stock and processing. His story ideas were original. His familiarity with the

209

Glasgow setting and Glasgow humour helped to shape his film. He benefited from its prestigious launching at the Edinburgh Film Festival. Cinema distribution and television screening in Britain gave him some revenue. It also led to the acceptance of other films, bigger (they could hardly be smaller!) production budgets and, with the help of David Puttnam, entry into the United States.

It could therefore be done. Could it be done again? Given the same perseverance it might. It is unlikely that there would be an equal response to what is twee in his film approach. But there are other styles in film-making that could be attractive to sources of finance. Even if the comedies remain the best-known products of Ealing Studios in the forties and fifties, there were other and different films of distinction. *Another Time, Another Place* showed that the Bill Forsyth Glasgow-oriented seam is not the only one worth opening up in Scotland.

It is never going to be easy to raise money for films in Scotland. In illustration of this John Grierson once compared the situation to that of the burghers of Calais who 'failed to fire a salute for the English King and were up, hats off, on the royal mat. They said they had seven good reasons to advance. They duly advanced them cogently and in great detail, one by one. The seventh was that they had no guns'. Grierson continued, 'Film-making belongs like all show business to that magical world in which two and two can make five, but also three and even less. It is, by that token, not a business to which the presbyterian mind is natively and nationally attuned'.

I do not think that that necessarily closes the door on the financing of Scottish feature films from Scottish and other sources. Edinburgh has the reputation of being one of the world's leading financial centres. It is not impossible to think of a gesture being made by an Angus Grossart, as indeed one was in the early years of Goldcrest. What Hugh Fraser did to launch Films of Scotland could be done again (although the arithmetic would need some upward adjusting). Courage and belief there would need to be. These are not dead in Scotland but it takes unsparing effort to engage them productively. I speak from experience.

Just as American distribution was a key factor in the financial formula in the post-war period, so television is today. Television has a monstrous appetite. A year's output from Scottish sources could satisfy it for no more than a day or two. The appetite will not grow less. With the threatened multiplicity of channels it is likely to increase. That does not necessarily mean an easy source of finance; but it does mean an expanding exposure, not a contracting one as in the cinemas. How to make films on Scottish subjects irresistible to television and to audiences in cinemas? This question is central to the whole issue of films of Scotland. It carries the potentially awkward corollary: Why should audiences furth of Scotland be attracted by anything Scottish?

Let me first excise some preconceptions. There was a time when the easiest way to establish Scottishness was to employ the familiar symbols: the kilt, the bagpipe, heather, whisky, haggis, Highland cattle and the thatched cottage by the lochside. That time has passed, although there are still film-makers overseas who have recourse to these symbols when they want to identify Scotland. Some of them have been surprised that we should wish to abandon a form of dress as distinctive as the kilt and a spectacle as stirring as massed pipe bands. The heat engendered in some Scottish quarters over this question has been unreasonably excessive.

There was a time also when such historical characters as Scott, Stevenson and Barrie would be quoted as sources. More recently Eric Linklater, Compton Mackenzie and Neil Gunn have been mentioned. Certainly Linklater's bubbling sense of fun in *Juan in America* could inspire a film-maker and entertain audiences on both sides of the Atlantic. Of Neil Gunn's work his most profound novels would be untranslatable in film terms. A screenplay does exist for *Morning Tide* (I have a copy) but its production was endlessly delayed by Robert Clark when he owned the rights. *Bloodhunt*, rejected by Sir John Davis at Rank, made an excellent television film. Laurence Henson hopes one day to make *Butcher's Broom*. BBC Scotland made a memorable production of Lewis Grassic Gibbon's trilogy *A Scots Quair*, lost to the cinema screen. Shots of the sky above the stark Mearns landscape transformed the story by introducing spiritualising elements to the theme.

Plays or novels attract producers because someone else has taken the initial risk of trying them out on the public. Among the literary successes of the past ten years has been Alasdair Gray's *Lanark*, on which the author has been at work preparing a screenplay. Iain Brown, its prospective producer, properly regarded it as a daunting prospect. William McIlvanney's Glasgow-based detective story, *Laidlaw*, originally written for Sean Connery and declined, is now with a Canadian company. The likeliest book to reach the screen is *Growing Up in the Gorbals*, Ralph Glasser's first volume of autobiography, with the experienced Karel Reisz as executive producer for Granada Film Productions.

Scotland has a limited flow of creative writing on which film-makers could draw. It would be much better in the long term (and you cannot be more optimistic than beginning to think of the long term) if there were writers who could express their ideas visually, as Bill Forsyth and Bill Douglas have done. John Byrne did so for his television series *Tutti Frutti* and enjoyed an immediacy of impact which might not have survived translation at second hand.

Film-makers in Scotland have never lacked for advice. Some of it came from wise older colleagues like Grierson with a lifetime of experience behind them. More often it came from academics, i.e. those with no practical experience of making films or of raising money to make them. It would have been surprising if the film-makers had not been irritated. They were, on a number of occasions when film-making in Scotland was under discussion, in all but the essential areas of money and ideas. I have yet to hear any workable project put forward at these sessions which would result in a worthwhile film about Scotland which audiences would pay to see.

A typical forum was the 'Scotch Reels' event at the 1982 Edinburgh Film Festival. It quickly became clear from many of the contributions that the conference was concerned more with the political content of the films than with the practicalities of finance. Tartanry and the Kailyard were inevitably targets. So also was what was called the 'Scotland on the Move' character of many of the productions of Films of Scotland. Political preoccupation can be as much justified as any other angled approach to film-making. One of the speakers emphasised the importance of 'prioritising' strategies for ideological intervention in the context of a national culture which he maintained had been systematically deformed. That may be so. What none of the contributors attempted to define was a strategy whereby 'oppositional practices' could be reflected in films made for entertainment on television or in the cinema, assuming that the film-makers would be prepared to give their work this political colour.

Resolution of the conflict between the academics and the film-makers was no nearer at the end of this conference than it had been at the beginning. They are still as far apart. As I have detailed in these pages, producers in Hollywood and London have over-exploited Tartanry and Kailyard in the representation of Scotland. As for the 'Scotland on the Move' criticism: the country was on the move at the time Films of Scotland put the movement on record and it seemed natural to make films about the major industrial and infrastructural changes of the day. It would be easier to give credence to this criticism if those advancing it would say what kind of films should have been made, how they would have been financed and what audiences would have welcomed seeing them. I share the irritation of the film-makers.

Grierson's advice was, as always, constructive.

> However small the country, however local the source of revelation, it is what is revealed in depth of what men have seen or felt or done that matters and, by and large, the language of revelation is a universal one, perhaps the only universal one. So I don't think that we are engaging in small or provincial affairs when we take thought of our own small country, for they are not necessarily so. It is only we who in the smallness of our observation make them small. Each town, each village, has its story of men made and something done. The arc of the sky over us is as wide as any, the land under has seen as much of the light and as much of the light of love as any.

I would like to see Scottish films draw on the here and now. By the time these words are in print someone will have made a film of the Piper Alpha disaster and of the heroism of those who rescued the survivors and quelled the flames. There is a *Blackboard Jungle* theme in what is happening in our schools today. There is another in the kind of road movie which the Australians made in *Travelling North*: a simple enough story but warmly human, with the Great North Road as a bonus. I would like to see Rikki Fulton's brilliant miming used to more demanding purpose, as happened with Fernandel in his Don Camillo films and Jacques Tati in *Jour de Fête*. There is a film in the conflict between afforestation and concern for the environment which surfaced in the controversy over the Caithness Flow Country. Can no one make a film as simple and universally appealing as Vittorio de Sica did in *Umberto D*? There are prototypes in plenty in our urban streets.

I give these only as random examples. They have nothing to do with Tartanry and the Kailyard (once defined by James Bridie as 'a cabbage patch which also supports hens. It smells a bit'). One of the speakers at the conference to which I have referred said that during the event the film-makers had been urged 'to get down to the essential truth about Scotland'. There was no essential truth, he protested. It did not exist. There were many truths. What was needed were more useful, valid, progressive images of the country. If these can be married to the will of the film-makers – and if there is willingness among financial institutions to make marriage possible – a Scottish cinema could still emerge.

I cited at the outset artists to give form to ideas as the third requirement. The film-making community in Scotland may not be large but it has men and women who are talented, dedicated and determined. They have graduated through documentary and, as I have shown, are now ready to make ambitious films for the cinemas and for television. This is an asset which should not be undervalued. Outside London there is no area of Britain which is better equipped to produce feature films.

It was the film-makers themselves who added a desirable facility. Paddy Higson, associate producer on a number of films for television and the cinema, was frustrated by the problems of making feature films in Scotland without a production base. She took the initiative in the conversion of a disused cinema in Glasgow into the Black Cat Studios. Finance was raised by her feature film company, Antonine Productions, with help from Singleton Holdings and the Scottish Development Agency. It had at one time been used by BBC

Scotland to record programmes but needed much upgrading. In a perfect world such enterprise would be rewarded with continuous use. Film-making, fluid and fluctuating, is not a perfect world.

Scottish films cannot prosper in a vacuum. Defeat at the Devolution Referendum in 1979 undoubtedly undermined national confidence in this as in other facets of national identity. As could be expected of him John Grierson put the point well when he gave the Celebrity Lecture at the Edinburgh Film Festival:

> We, in Scotland, have a special reason to consider the relationship between the loss of public confidence and the lack of support for our national film-makers. To be short about it, support for our national film-makers barely exists, nor does the political power seem to care a whit whether support exists or not. We have a country of five million people, larger than many represented separately in the United Nations. We have a culture which we consider natively distinct and our own. We have certainly a concern for our self-esteem which we find proper and necessary. Those are, in effect, the important intangibles by which we live and move and have our being. Yet, to put it plainly, we are thwarted in the expression of these intangibles by which we live and move and have our being. We are denied access to the means of production by which we can give expression to our self-esteem and draw from it an inspiration for the present and the future.

At the end of the day so much depends on the will of the film-makers themselves. It is a living force in Scotland and will not be suppressed. Whatever is done, let it be done with confidence and some pride. No more cringing and whingeing, no more finding excuses and avoiding issues. Scotland is a splendid country, a God-given gift to film-makers in the range of its scenery, magnificent in the Highlands and islands, full of variety around the coast and rich in contrast in the cities. I believe too that the film-makers have only begun to mine the resource which is the Scottish character. There more than anywhere else can they bring the transforming power of revelation to bear.

Filmography

ANNIE LAURIE (1927)
Production: Jury-Metro-Goldwyn. *Direction*: John S. Robertson.
With Lillian Gish, Norman Kerry, Creighton Hale, Hobart Bosworth, Russell Simpson, David Torrence, Patricia Avery. (89 mins.)

ANOTHER TIME, ANOTHER PLACE (1983)
Production: Umbrella Films. *Producer*: Simon Perry. *Screenplay and direction*: Michael Radford. From the novel by Jessie Kesson. *Associate producer*: Paul Cowan. *Executive producer*: Timothy Burrill. *Photgraphy*: Roger Deakins. *Editing*: Tom Priestley. *Music*: John McLeod. Neapolitan music arranged by Corrado Sfogli and Giovanni Mauriello of the Nuova Compagnia di Canto Popolare. *Art direction*: Hayden Pearce.
With Phyllis Logan, Gian Luca Favilla, Paul Young, Tom Watson, Denise Coffey, Carol Ann Crawford, Scott Johnston, Giovanni Mauriello, Claudio Rosini, Gregor Fisher, Jennifer Piercey, Yvonne Gilan, Ray Jeffries. (101 mins.)

AS LONG AS YOU'RE YOUNG (1962)
Production: Glasgow Films. *Producer*: David Welsh. *Direction and Photography*: Edward McConnell. Commentary written by George Bruce and spoken by Bryden Murdoch. *Music*: Stanley Thompson. (25 mins.)

BATTLE OF THE SEXES (1959)
Production: Bryanston. *Producer*: Monja Danischewsky. *Direction*: Charles Crichton. From a story *The Catbird Seat* by James Thurber.
With Peter Sellers, Constance Cummings, Robert Morley, Jameson Clark, Moultrie Kelsall, Alex Mackenzie, Roddy Macmillan, James Gibson. (84mins.)

BIG BANANA FEET (1976)
Production: Viz. Unicorn Enterprises. *Producer*: Patrick Higson. *Direction*: Murray Grigor. *Photography*: David Peat. *Sound*: Ian Leslie.
With Billy Connolly. (77 mins.)

BLOOD RED ROSES (1986)
Production: 7:84 Theatre Company. *Producer*: Steve Clark-Hall. *Script and direction*: John McGrath. *Photography*: Mark Littlewood. *Editors*: Jane Wood, Jo Nott.
With Elizabeth Maclennan, James Grant, Gregor Fisher, Dawn Archibald. (140 mins.)

BONNIE PRINCE CHARLIE (1946-47)
Production: London Films. *Producer*: Edward Black. *Direction*: Anthony Kimmins. *Screenplay*: Clemence Dane. *Photography*: Robert Krasker. *Art direction*: Vincent Korda,

Wilfred Shingleton, J. Bato. *Costumes*: George K. Benda. *Exterior photography*: Osmond Borrodaile. Music composed by Ian Whyte, played by the London Film Symphony Orchestra, conducted by Hubert Clifford. *Historical advisers*: Cyril Hartman, A.E. Haswell-Miller.

With David Niven, Margaret Leighton, Jack Hawkins, Judy Campbell, Finlay Currie, Ronald Adam, Morland Graham, Elwyn Brook-Jones, John Laurie, Hugh Kelly, Hector Ross, Franklin Dyall, Guy Lefeuvre, Nell Ballantyne, Henry Oscar, Bruce Seton. (118 mins.)

BONNIE SCOTLAND (1935)
Producer: Hal E. Roach. *Direction*: James W. Horne.
With Stan Laurel, Oliver Hardy, Anne Grey, Daphne Pollard. (80 mins.)

THE BRAVE DON'T CRY (1952)
Production: Group 3. *Producer*: John Grierson. *Direction*: Philip Leacock.
Screenplay: Montagu Slater. *Photography*: Arthur Grant. *Editing*: John Trumper.
With John Gregson, Meg Buchanan, John Rae, Fulton Mackay, Andrew Keir, Wendy Noel, Russell Waters, Jameson Clark, Eric Woodburn, Jean Anderson, Archie Duncan. (90 mins.)

BRIDAL PATH (1959)
Production: Sidney Gilliat and Frank Launder. *Associate producer*: Leslie Gilliat.
Direction: Frank Launder. *Screenplay*: Frank Launder, Geoffrey Willans, from the novel by Nigel Tranter. *Photography*: Arthur Ibbetson. *Editing*: Geoffrey Foot. *Art direction*: Wilfred Shingleton. *Music*: Cedric Thorpe Davie. *Songs*: Campbeltown Gaelic Choir.
With Bill Travers, Fiona Clyne, George Cole, Gordon Jackson, Dilys Laye, Duncan Macrae, Charlotte Mitchell, Alex Mackenzie, Eric Woodburn, Jack Lambert.
(95 mins.)

BRIGADOON (1954)
Production: Metro-Goldwyn-Mayer. *Producer*: Arthur Freed. *Direction*: Vincente Minnelli. *Screenplay*: Alan Jay Lerner. *Music*: Frederick Loewe. *Choreography*: Gene Kelly. *Photography*: Joseph Ruttenberg.
With Gene Kelly, Van Johnson, Cyd Charisse, Elaine Stewart, Barry Jones, Hugh Laing, Albert Sharpe, Virginia Bosler, Jimmy Thompson, Tudor Owen, Owen McGiveney, Dee Turnell, Dody Heath, Eddie Quillan. (102 mins.)

THE BROTHERS (1947)
Production: Triton Films, Gainsborough Studios. *Producer*: Sydney Box.
Direction: David MacDonald. From the novel by L.A.G. Strong.
Photography: Stephen Dade. Music composed by Cedric Thorpe Davie. *Musical director*: Muir Mathieson.
With Patricia Roc, Will Fyffe, Maxwell Reed, Finlay Currie, Duncan Macrae, Morland Graham, Andrew Crawford, Donald MacAlister, John Laurie, Jack Lambert, James Woodburn, David Keir, Megs Jenkins, Patrick Boxhill. (98 mins.)

Scotland in Film

CHARIOTS OF FIRE (1981)
Production: Enigma, for 20th Century-Fox and Allied Stars. *Producer*: David Puttnam.
Direction: Hugh Hudson. *Screenplay*: Colin Welland. *Photography*: David Watkin.
Editing: Terry Rawlings. *Art direction*: Anna Ridley, Jonathan Amberston, Len
Huntingford, Andrew Sanders. *Music*: Vangelis Papathanassiou. *Editing*: Terry
Rawlings.
With Ian Charleson, Ben Cross, Nigel Havers, Nicholas Farrell, Daniel Gerroll, Cheryl
Campbell, John Gielgud, Lindsay Anderson, Nigel Davenport, Ian Holm, Patrick
Magee, David Yelland, Peter Egan, John Young, Gerry Slevin, Wallace Campbell.
(121 mins.)

THE CHEVIOT, THE STAG AND THE BLACK BLACK OIL (1974)
Production: 7:84 Theatre Company. *Producer*: Graeme McDonald. *Direction*: John
Mackenzie. *Photography*: Brian Tufano. *Editing*: Gordon Clarke. *Script editor*: Ann
Scott. *Designer*: Barry Newbery.
With John Bett, David Maclennan, Dolina Maclennan, Elizabeth Maclennan, Timothy
Martin, Alex Norton, Bill Paterson, Allan Ross, John Byrne, John McGrath, Charles
Kearney, James Cosmo, Stuart Mungall, Terry Cavers, Ian Glas, David Steuart,
Kenneth Benda, Kevin Collins. (123 mins.)

CHILDREN OF THE CITY (1944)
Production: Paul Rotha Productions. *Script and direction*: Budge Cooper.
Photography: Wolfgang Suschitzky. (20 mins.)

CLYDESCOPE (1974)
Production: Viz. *Script and direction*: Murray Grigor. *Photography*: David Peat.
Editing: Patrick Higson. *Narration*: Michael MacLiammoir. *Songs*: Billy Connolly.
Music composed by Ron Geesin. *Animation*: John Patrick Byrne, Donald Holwill.
With Billy Connolly, Stephen and Liz Yardley, Peter Behrens, Bill Paterson,
Christopher Higson. (31 mins.)

COMFORT AND JOY (1984)
Production: Columbia-EMI-Warner. *Producers*: Davina Belling, Clive Parsons. *Script
and direction*: Bill Forsyth. *Photography*: Chris Menges. *Editing*: Michael Ellis.
Production designer: Adrienne Atkinson. *Art direction*: Andy Harris. *Music*: Mark
Knopfler. *Jingles*: Andy Park.
With Bill Paterson, Eleanor David, C.P. Grogan, Alex Norton, Patrick Malahide,
Roberto Bernardi, George Rossi, Peter Rossi, Billy McElhaney. (90 mins.)

CROFTERS (1944)
Production: Greenpark Unit of Verity Films. *Associate producer*: Edgar Anstey. *Script
and direction*: Ralph Keene. *Photography*: Peter Hennessy. *Editing*: Denis Hopper.
Music: Denis Blood. Orchestra directed by John Hollingsworth. (20 mins.)

CULLODEN (1964)
Production: BBC. *Producer*: Peter Watkins. *Script and direction*: Peter Watkins.
Photography: Dick Bush. *Music and sound*: John Gatland and Lou Hanks. (70 mins.)

218

Filmography

DEATH WATCH (La Mort en direct) (1979)
Production: Selta Film, Little Bear, Sara Film, Gaumont/Atenne 2 (Paris), TV 15 (Munich). *Executive producer*: Jean Serge Breton. *Co-production and direction*: Bertrand Tavernier. *Location unit manager*: Iain Smith. *Script*: David Rayfiel and Bertrand Tavernier. Based on the novel *The Continuous Katherine Mortenhoe* by David Compton. *Photography*: Pierre-William Glenn. *Editing*: Armand Psenny, Michael Ellis. *Music*: Antoine Duhamel. *Musical direction*: Harry Rabinovitz.
With Romy Schneider, Harvey Keitel, Harry Dean Stanton, Max Von Sydow, Therese Liotard, Caroline Langrishe, William Russel, Vadim Glowna, Eva Maria Meineke, Bernard Wicki, Boyd Nelson, Jake D'Arcy, Paul Young, John Shedden, Robbie Coltrane. (130 mins.)

DR JEKYLL AND MR HYDE (1932)
Production: Paramount. *Producer and director*: Rouben Mamoulian.
Screenplay: Samuel Hoffenstein and Percy Heath. *Art direction*: Hans Dreier.
Photography: Karl Struss.
With Fredric March, Miriam Hopkins, Rose Hobart, Holmes Herbert, Halliwell Hobbes, Edgar Norton. (98 mins.)

DR JEKYLL AND MR HYDE (1941)
Production: Metro-Goldwyn-Mayer. *Producer and director*: Victor Fleming.
Screenplay: John Lee Mahin. *Art direction*: Cedric Gibbons. *Photography*: Joseph Ruttenberg. *Music*: Frank Waxman.
With Spencer Tracy, Ingrid Bergman, Lana Turner, Donald Crisp, Ian Hunter, Marton MacLane, C. Aubrey Smith, Sara Allgood, Billy Bevan. (127 mins.)

DRIFTERS (1929)
Production: EMB Film Unit. *Producer, director, script and editing*: John Grierson.
Photography: Basil Emmott. (40 mins.)

THE DUNA BULL (1972)
Production: IFA (Scotland). *Direction*: Laurence Henson. *Script*: Clifford Hanley. From an idea by Forsyth Hardy. *Photography*: Edward McConnell. Music composed by Frank Spedding, conducted by Marcus Dods.
With Juliet Cadzow, Richard Harbord, Victor Carin, Willie Joss, Tom Watson, Mary Riggans, James Cosmo, Martin Cochrane, James Mackenzie, Jean Taylor-Smith, Alex McCrindle, John Young, Roy Boutcher, Dudley Stuart-White. (33 mins.)

THE EDGE OF THE WORLD (1937)
Production: Rock Studios. *Producer*: Joe Rock. *Script and direction*: Michael Powell.
Photography: Ernest Palmer, Skeets Kelly, Monty Berman. *Musical direction*: Cyril Ray. *Choral effects*: The Women of the Glasgow Orpheus Choir. *Orchestrations*: W.L. Williamson.

Scotland in Film

With John Laurie, Belle Crystall, Eric Berry, Kitty Kirwan, Finlay Currie, Niall MacGinnis, Grant Sutherland, Campbell Robson, George Summers, and all the people of the island of Foula. (81 mins.)

ENCHANTED ISLES (1957)
Production: Anglo-Scottish Pictures. *Script*: Tom Twigg. Music arranged by Cedric Thorpe Davie.
Commentary written by Alan Campbell MacLean and spoken by Fulton Mackay.
(17 mins.)

THE EDINBURGH FESTIVAL (1966)
Production: Campbell Harper Films. *Sound*: Anvil Films (Scotland). Commentary written and spoken by Tom Fleming.
Art exhibitions: Soutine, Modiglioni, Indian Art, John Maxwell, Sidney Nolan. Shakespeare Exhibition. Yehudi Menuhin, Michael Roll. The Scottish National Orchestra, conducted by Alexander Gibson. Theatre Workshop in Shakespeare's *Henry IV*. The Stuttgart Theatre Ballet in *Quintet*. Opera of the National Theatre, Prague, in *Dalibor*. *Chaganog* with Julian Chagrin, George Ogilvie. Les Ballets Africains The National Company of Guinea. Military Tattoo. (29 mins.)

THE FACE OF SCOTLAND (1938)
Production: Realist Film Unit. *Direction*: Basil Wright. *Photography*: A.E. Jeakins. *Music*: Walter Leigh. (20 mins.)

FESTIVAL IN EDINBURGH (1955)
Production: Associated British-Pathe. *Direction*: Douglas Clarke. *Photography*: Jo Jago. Musical direction by Muir Mathieson. Commentary written by Robert Kemp and spoken by Alastair Sim. (14 mins.)

FLESH AND BLOOD (1951)
An Anatole de Grunwald Production for London Films. *Direction*: Anthony Kimmins. *Screenplay*: Anatole de Grunwald, from the play *The Sleeping Clergyman* by James Bridie. *Photography*: Otto Heller. *Editing*: G. Turney-Smith. *Art direction*: Paul Sheriff. *Music*: Charles Williams.
With Richard Todd, Glynis Johns, Joan Greenwood, André Morell, Ursula Howells, Freda Jackson, George Cole, James Hayter, Ronald Howard, Muriel Aked.
(102 mins.)

FLOODTIDE (1949)
Production: Aquila. *Direction*: Frederick Wilson. *Script*: Donald B. Wilson, Frederick Wilson and George Blake. *Photography*: George Stretton. *Music*: Robert Irving.
With Gordon Jackson, Rona Anderson, John Laurie, Jack Lambert. (90 mins.)

THE GARDEN BEYOND (1977)
Production: Breck Film Productions. Written and produced by Douglas Eadie. *Direction*: Brian Crumlish. *Photography*: Mick Campbell. *Editing*: Fiona Macdonald. *Music*: Owen Hand.

Filmography

With Bertie Scott, Henry Stamper, Bill Paterson, Gerry Slevin, Sharon Erskine, Betty Gillin, Ian Ireland, Martin Black, Ronnie Letham, John Sheddon, John Young, Frances Low. (55 mins.)

GEORDIE (1955)
A Launder-Gilliat Production. *Direction*: Frank Launder. *Screenplay*: Sidney Gilliat and Frank Launder. *Photography*: Wilkie Cooper. *Art direction*: Norman Arnold. *Music*: William Alwyn, conducted by Muir Matheson.
With Alastair Sim, Bill Travers, Paul Young, Norah Gorsen, Anna Ferguson, Miles Malleson, Brian Reece, Raymond Huntley, Doris Goddard, Jameson Clark, Molly Urquhart, Jack Radcliffe. (99 mins.)

THE GHOST GOES WEST (1935)
Production: London Films. *Producer*: Alexander Korda. *Direction*: René Clair.
With Robert Donat, Jean Parker, Eugene Pallette, Hay Petrie. (90 mins.)

THE GIRL IN THE PICTURE (1986)
Production: Antonine Productions. *Producer*: Paddy Higson. *Script and direction*: Cary Parker. *Production supervisor*: Alan J. Wands. *Production co-ordinator*: Alison Campbell. *Photography*: Dick Pope. *Editing*: Bert Eeles.
With Gordon John Sinclair, Irina Brook, David MacKay, Gregor Fisher, Caroline Guthrie, Paul Young, Rikki Fulton. (91 mins.)

GLASGOW 1980 (1980)
Production: Ogam Films. *Direction*: Oscar Marzaroli. *Photography*: Martin Singleton. *Script and commentary*: Douglas Eadie. *Narration*: Michael Harrigan. *Editing*: Bill Forsyth. (30 mins.)

GLASGOW BELONGS TO ME (1966)
Production: IFA (Scotland) for British Transport Films.
Direction: Laurence Henson. *Photography*: Edward McConnell. (17 mins.)

THE GORBALS STORY (1950)
Production: Eros Films, Merton Park Studios. *Direction and screenplay*: David MacKane. *Photography*: Stanley Clinton.
With Russell Hunter, Archie Duncan, Roddy Macmillan, Betty Henderson, Howard Connell, Marjorie Thomson. (74 mins.)

THE GREAT MILL RACE (1975)
Production: Edinburgh Film Productions. *Direction*: Robin Crichton. *Associate producer*: Mike Pavett. *Screenplay*: Alasdair Gray and Clifford Hanley.
Photography: David MacDonald, David Peat, Peter Warrilow. Music composed by Frank Spedding, conducted by Marcus Dods.
With John Cairney, Russell Hunter, John Grieve, Leonard Maguire, Jonty Miller, Ros Drinkwater, Elizabeth Brown, Walter Carr, Brown Derby, Michael Elder, John

221

Young, Jack Angus, Hugh Boyle, Maureen Jack, Rose MacBain, Nan Norman, and stuntman, Jim Boyce. (32 mins.)

GREGORY'S GIRL (1980)
Production: Lake Film Productions. *Producers*: Davina Belling, Clive Parsons. *Direction and script*: Bill Forsyth. *Photography*: Michael Coulter. *Editing*: John Gow. *Art direction*: Adrienne Atkinson. *Music*: Colin Tully.
With Gordon John Sinclair, Dee Hepburn, Jake D'Arcy, Claire Grogan, Robert Buchanan, William Greenlees, Alan Love, Caroline Guthrie, Carol Macartney, Douglas Sannachan, Allison Forster, Chic Murray, Alex Norton, John Bett, David Anderson, Billy Feeley, Maeve Watt, Muriel Romanes, Patrick Lewsley. (91 mins.)

HALLAIG (1984)
Production: The Island House Film and Video Workshop. *Producer*: Timothy Neat. *Photography*: Mark Littlewood. *Sound*: Ian Leslie. *Rostrum camera*: Donald Holwill. *Editing*: Russell Fenton.
Consultants: Hamish Henderson, John MacInnes, Catriona Montgomery, Murray Grigor, John Berger. (66 mins.)

THE HAND OF ADAM (1975)
Production: Viz. *Script and direction*: Murray Grigor. *Architectural and historical adviser*: A.A. Tait. *Photography*: David Peat, Mike Coulter, Jon Schorstein. *Editing*: Patrick Higson. *Narration*: Robert Trotter. *Production*: Iain Smith. Music composed by Frank Spedding and conducted by Marcus Dods. (33 mins.)

THE HEART IS HIGHLAND (1952)
Production: British Transport Films. *Producer*: Edgar Anstey. *Associate producer*: Stewart McAllister. *Direction*: John Taylor. *Photography*: Ronald Craigen and Reg Hughes. *Editing*: John Legard. *Music*: Cedric Thorpe Davie. Commentary written and spoken by Moray McLaren. (22 mins.)

THE HEART OF SCOTLAND (1962)
Production: Templar Film Studios. *Direction*: Laurence Henson. From an outline treatment by John Grierson. *Photography*: Edward McConnell. Commentary written by John Ormond and spoken by Bryden Murdoch. Music composed by Frank Spedding and conducted by Marcus Dods. (24 mins.)

HEAVENLY PURSUITS (1986)
Production: Island and Skreba. *Producer*: Michael Relph. *Script and direction*: Charles Gormley. *Photography*: Michael Coulter. *Music*: B.A. Robertson.
With Tom Conti, Helen Mirren. (92 mins.)

HERO (1982)
Production: Maya Films (Scotland). *Producer*: Andrew St. John. *Script and direction*: Barney Platts-Mills. *Photography*: Adam Barker-Mill. *Music*: Paul Steen.

With Alastair Kenneil, Derek McGuire, Caroline Kenneil, Steven Hamilton, Stuart Grant, Aonghas MacNiecall. (90 mins.)

HIGHLANDER (1986)
Producers: Peter Davis, William Panzer. *Direction*: Russell Mulcahy.
Screenplay: Gregory Widen, Peter Bell, Larry Ferguson. *Photography*: Gerry Fisher. *Music*: Michael Kamen.
With Christopher Lambert, Sean Connery, Roxanne Hart, Clancy Brown.
(110 mins.)

I KNOW WHERE I'M GOING (1944)
Production: The Archers. Written, produced and directed by Michael Powell and Emeric Pressburger. *Associate producer*: George R. Busby. *Photography*: Erwin Hillier. *Editing*: John Seabourne. *Art direction*: Alfred Junge. *Music*: Allan Gray.
With Wendy Hiller, Roger Livesey, George Carney, Pamela Brown, Walter Hudd, Captain Duncan MacKechnie, Ian Sadler, Finlay Currie, Murdo Morrison, Margot Fitzsimmons, Captain C.W.R. Knight, Donald Strachan, John Rae, Duncan MacIntyre, Jean Cadell, Norman Shelley, Petula Clark, Catherine Lacey, Valentine Dyall, Kitty Kirwan, John Laurie, Graham Moffat. (92 mins.)

ILL FARES THE LAND (1982)
Production: Portman Productions for Scottish and Global TV Enterprises and Channel 4. *Screenplay and direction*: Bill Bryden. *Producer*: Robert Love. *Associate producer*: Dickie Bamber. *Photography*: John Coquillon. *Editing*: Lesley Walker. *Production designers*: Ken Bridgeman, Ray Simm. *Music*: John Tams.
With Joseph Brady, James Copeland, J.G. Devlin, Ron Donachie, Neil Duncan, James Ellis, James Grant, Roy Hanlon, David Hayman, Morag Hood, Robert James, William MacBain, Erika MacInnes, George MacInnes, Fulton Mackay, Donnie MacLean, Andrew McCullough, Brian Pettifer, John Shedden, Robert Stephens, Ewan Stewart, Jean Taylor-Smith, Valerie Whittington, Jan Wilson. (104 mins.)

JUST ANOTHER SATURDAY (1975)
Production: BBC 1. *Producer*: Graeme McDonald. *Direction*: John Mackenzie.
Script: Peter McDougall. *Script editor*: Ann Scott. *Photography*: Phil Meheux.
With John Morrison, Eileen McCallum, Bill Henderson, Ken Hutchinson, Billy Connolly, Jim Gibb, Phil McCall, Jake D'Arcy, James Walsh, Martin Black.
(77 mins.)

KIDNAPPED (1959)
Production: Walt Disney. *Producer*: Walt Disney. *Associate producer*: Hugh Attwooll. *Direction*: Robert Stevenson. *Screenplay*: Robert Stevenson, from the novel by Robert Louis Stevenson. *Photography*: Paul Beeson. *Editing*: Gordon Stone. *Art direction*: Carmen Dillon. *Costume design*: Margaret Furse. *Music*: Cedric Thorpe Davie, directed by Muir Mathieson.
With Peter Finch, James MacArthur, Bernard Lee, John Laurie, Niall MacGinnis, Finlay Currie, Peter O'Toole, Miles Malleson, Oliver Johnston, Duncan Macrae,

Andrew Cruickshank, Alex Mackenzie, Norman MacOwan, Eileen Way, Jack Stewart, Edie Martin, Abe Barker. (95 mins.)

THE KIDNAPPERS (1953)
A Nolbandov-Parkyn Production. *Direction*: Philip Leacock. *Screenplay*: Neil Paterson. *Photography*: Eric Cross. *Art direction*: Edward Carrick. *Editing*: John Trumper. Music composed by Bruce Montgomery, played by the Royal Philharmonic Orchestra, conducted by Muir Mathieson.
With Duncan Macrae, Jean Anderson, Adrienne Corri, Theodore Bikel, Jon Whiteley, Vincent Winter, Francis de Wolff, James Sutherland, John Rae, Jack Stewart, Jameson Clark, Eric Woodburn, Christopher Beeny, Howard Connell. (93 mins.)

A KIND OF SEEING (1967)
Production: IFA (Scotland). *Direction and photography*: Edward McConnell.
Music: Frank Spedding. (13 mins.)

THE LAND OF ROBERT BURNS (1956)
Production: British Transport Films. *In charge of production*: Edgar Anstey.
Producer: Stewart McAllister. *Script*: Maurice Lindsay. *Direction*: Joe Mendoza.
Photography: Robert Paynter. *Editing*: Margot Fleischner. *Music director*: Cedric Thorpe Davie. *Sound recording*: Ken Cameron. (21 mins.)

LAXDALE HALL (1952)
Production: Group 3. *Executive producer*: John Grierson. *Direction*: John Eldridge.
Script: John Eldridge and Alfred Shaughnessy, from the novel by Eric Linklater.
Photography: Arthur Grant.
With Ronald Squire, Kathleen Ryan, Raymond Huntley, Sebastian Shaw, Fulton Mackay, Roddy Macmillan, Jameson Clark, Andrew Keir. (77 mins.)

A LINE FOR ALL SEASONS (1981)
Production: IFA (Scotland). *Producer*: Laurence Henson. *Script*: Laurence Henson.
Direction and photography: Edward McConnell. (30 mins.)

THE LINE TO SKYE (1973)
Production: IFA (Scotland). *Direction and photography*: Edward McConnell.
Commentary: William McIlvanney. *Narration*: John Shedden.
Music: Muir Mathieson. (15 mins.)

THE LITTLE MINISTER (1934)
Production: RKO. *Direction*: Richard Wallace. From the novel by J.M. Barrie.
With Katharine Hepburn, John Beal, Alan Hale, Donald Crisp, Lumsden Hare, Andy Clyde, Beryl Mercer, Frank Conroy, Mary Gordon, Reginald Denny. (110 mins.)

LIVING APART TOGETHER (1983)
Production: Legion Productions. *Producers*: Gavrick Losey, Paddy Higson. *Screenplay and direction*: Charles Gormley. *Photography*: Mark Littlewood. *Editing*: Patrick

Filmography

Higson. *Art direction*: Adrienne Atkinson. *Music*: B.A. Robertson.
With B.A. Robertson, Barbara Kellermann, Judi Trott, David Anderson, Jimmy
Logan, Amy Walls, Ben Walls, James Cosmo, William Elliott, Kathy Brawley,
George McGowan Bank, Peter Capaldi, Anne Kristen.   (88 mins.)

LOCAL HERO (1983)

Production: Enigma Productions. *Producer*: David Puttnam. *Script and direction*: Bill
Forsyth. *Photography*: Chris Menges. *Editing*: Michael Bradsell. *Production
designer*: Roger Murray-Leach. *Art direction*: Adrienne Atkinson, Frank Walsh,
Ian Watson, Richard James. *Music*: Mark Knopfler.
With Burt Lancaster, Peter Riegert, Denis Lawson, Peter Capaldi, Fulton Mackay,
Christopher Rozycki, Jenny Seagrove, Jennifer Black, Christopher Asante, Rikki
Fulton, Alex Norton, Norman Chancer, David Anderson, Sandra Voe, Tam Dean
Burn, Kenny Ireland, Jimmy Yuill, James Kennedy, Charles Kearney, Willie Joss,
John Poland, John Gordon Sinclair, Ray Jeffries, Jonathan Watson, Caroline Guthrie,
Anne Scott Jones.   (111 mins.)

LOCH LOMOND (1967)

Production: IFA (Scotland). *Direction*: Laurence Henson. *Photography*: Edward
McConnell. *Commentary*: William McIlvanney. *Narration*: Alec Clunes. Music
composed by Frank Spedding, conducted by Marcus Dods.   (29 mins.)

THE LOVES OF ROBERT BURNS (1930)

Production: British and Dominions. *Direction*: Herbert Wilcox. *Script*: Herbert Wilcox,
Reginald Berkeley. *Photography*: David Kesson.
With Joseph Hislop, Dorothy Seacombe, Eve Grey, Craighall Sherry, Neil
Kenyon.   (95 mins.)

MACBETH (1948)

A Mercury Production. *Direction*: Orson Welles. From the play by William
Shakespeare. *Associate producer*: Richard Wilson. *Photography*: John L. Russell.
Editing: Louis Lindsay. *Art direction*: Fred Ritter. *Music*: Jacques Ibert.
With Orson Welles, Jeanette Nolan, Dan O'Herlihy, Roddy McDowall, Edgar
Barrier, Alan Napier, Erskine Sanford, John Dierkes, Keene Curtis, Peggy Webber,
Laurence Tuttle, Brainerd Duffield, Charles Lederer, Christopher Welles, Morgan
Farley, George Chirello.   (86 mins.)

MACBETH (1972)

Production: Playboy Productions / Caliban Films. *Executive producer*: Hugh M.
Hefner. *Producer*: Andrew Braunsberg. *Associate producer*: Timothy Burrill.
Direction: Roman Polanski. *Assistant director*: Simon Relph. *Screenplay*: Roman
Polanski and Kenneth Tynan, from the play by William Shakespeare.
Photography: Gilbert Taylor. *Editing*: Alastair McIntyre.
Production designer: Wilfred Shingleton.

225

With Jon Finch, Francesca Annis, Martin Shaw, Paul Shelley, Terence Bayler, Andrew Laurence, Frank Wylie, Bernard Archard, Bruce Purchase, Keith Chegwin, Noel Davis, Noelle Rimmington, Maisie MacFarquhar, Elsie Taylor, Vic Abbott, Diane Fletcher. (140 mins.)

MACKINTOSH (1968)

Production: IFA (Scotland). *Direction and script*: Murray Grigor. *Photography*: Edward McConnell. *Editing*: Bill Forsyth. *Narration*: Maurice Roeves. Music composed by Frank Spedding, conducted by Marcus Dods. *Graphics*: Averil McInwraith.

(30 mins.)

MADELEINE (1949)

A David Lean Production for Cineguild. *Producer*: Stanley Haynes. *Direction*: David Lean. *Screenplay*: Nicholas Phipps and Stanley Haynes. *Photography*: Guy Green. *Editing*: Geoffrey Foot. *Art direction*: John Bryan. *Costumes*: Margaret Furse. *Music*: William Alwyn.

With Ann Todd, Ivan Desny, Norman Wooland, Leslie Banks, Elizabeth Sellars, Jean Cadell, Eugene Deckers, Barry Jones, André Morell, Kynaston Reeves.

(114 mins.)

THE MAGGIE (1954)

Production: Ealing Studios-Michael Balcon. *Producer*: Michael Truman. Screenplay by William Rose, from an original story by Alexander Mackendrick. *Direction*: Alexander Mackendrick. *Photography*: Gordon Dines. *Editing*: Peter Tanner. *Art direction*: Jim Morahan. *Music*: John Addison.

With Paul Douglas, Alex Mackenzie, James Copeland, Abe Barker, Tommy Kearins, Hubert Gregg, Geoffrey Keen, Dorothy Alison, Andrew Keir, Meg Buchanan, Mark Dignam, Jameson Clark, Moultrie Kelsall, Fiona Clyde, Sheila Shand Gibbs.

(92 mins.)

MARY OF SCOTLAND (1936)

Production: R.K.O. *Producer*: Pandro S. Berman. *Direction*: John Ford. Screenplay by Dudley Nichols, based on the play by Maxwell Anderson. *Photography*: Joseph H. August. *Art direction*: Van Nest Polglase. *Editing*: Jane Loring. *Music*: Max Steiner, directed by Nathaniel Shilkret.

With Katharine Hepburn, Fredric March, Florence Eldridge, Douglas Walton, John Carradine, Robert Barrat, Gavin Muir, Ian Keith, Moroni Olsen, Ralph Forbes, Alan Mowbray, Freda Inescort, Donald Crisp, David Torrence, Cyril McLaglen, Wilfred Lucas, Robert Warwick. (123 mins.)

MARY QUEEN OF SCOTS (1972)

A Hal Wallis Production. *Producer*: Hal B. Wallis. *Direction*: Charles Jarrott. *Screenplay*: John Hale. *Photography*: Christopher Challis. Music composed and conducted by John Barry. *Production designer*: Terence Marsh. *Art direction*: Robert Cartwright. *Editing*: Richard Marden. *Costumes*: Margaret Furse.

With Vanessa Redgrave, Glenda Jackson, Patrick McGoohan, Timothy Dalton,

Nigel Davenport, Trevor Howard, Daniel Massey, Ian Holm, Andrew Keir, Tom
Fleming.   (128 mins.)

THE MASTER OF BALLANTRAE (1953)
Production: Warner Brothers. *Direction*: William Keighley. From the novel by Robert
Louis Stevenson.
With Errol Flynn, Roger Livesey, Anthony Steel, Beatrice Campbell, Felix Aylmer,
Mervyn Johns, Jacques Berthier, Yvonne Furneaux, Charles Goldner, Ralph Truman,
Francis de Wolff, Moultrie Kelsall, Charles Carson, Gillian Lynne, Archie Duncan,
Jack Lambert, John Wynne, Harry Herbert, Jack Taylor, Stephen Vercoe. (88 mins.)

MY CHILDHOOD (1972)
Production: BFI Production Board. *Producer*: Geoffrey Evans. *Direction and script*: Bill
Douglas. *Photography*: Mick Campbell. *Editor*: Brand Thumin.   (48 mins.)

MY AIN FOLK (1973)
Production: BFI Production Board. *Producer*: Nick Nacht. *Direction and script*: Bill
Douglas. *Photography*: Gale Tattersall, Bob Taylor. *Editing*: Peter West.   (55 mins.)

MY WAY HOME (1978)
Production: BFI Production Board. *Direction and script*: Bill Douglas. *Production
supervision*: Judy Cottam, Richard Craven. *Photography*: Ray Orton, Bob Taylor, Jess
Strasburg, Steve Shaw, Abdul and Ali. *Editing*: Mick Audsley. *Art direction*: Oliver
Bouchier, Elsie Restorick.
With Stephen Archibald, Hugh Restorick, Jean Taylor-Smith, Karl Fieseler, Bernard
McKenna, Paul Kermack, Helena Gloag, Ann Smith, Eileen McCullum, Helen
Crummy, John Crummy, Helen Eccles, John Eccles, Jessie Combe, William Carroll,
Anne McLeod, Robert Hendry, Miss Cameron (*My Ain Folk*), John Downey, Morag
McNee (*My Way Home*), Lennox Milne (*My Way Home*), Gerald James, John Young,
Ian Spowart, Sheila Scott, Rebecca Haddick, Joseph Blatchley.   (78 mins.)

NIGHT MAIL (1936)
Production: GPO Film Unit. *Producer*: John Grierson. *Direction*: Harry Watt and Basil
Wright. *Photography*: Jonah Jones, Chick Fowle. *Sound direction*: Alberto Cavalcanti.
Music: Benjamin Britten. *Verse*: W.H. Auden.   (30 mins.)

NORTH-EAST CORNER (1946)
Production: Greenpark Productions. *Producer*: Ralph Keene. *Direction*: John Eldridge.
Script: John R. Allan and Laurie Lee. *Music*: Kenneth Pakeman.   (20 mins.)

NORTH SEA (1938)
Production: GPO Film Unit. *Producer*: Alberto Cavalcanti. *Direction*: Harry Watt.
Photography: Jonah Jones and Chick Fowle.   (30 mins)

PERTHSHIRE PANORAMA (1959)
Production: Anglo-Scottish Pictures. *Direction and photography*: Bernard Davies.

Editing: Ben Hopkins. *Music*: Arthur Blake. Commentary written by Neil Peterson
and spoken by David Steuart.   (22 ins.)

THE PRACTICAL ROMANTIC – SIR WALTER SCOTT (1969)
Production: Anvil Films (Scotland). *Direction*: Hans Nieter. *Treatment and
commentary*: George Bruce. *Photography*: Adrian Jeakins. *Narration*: Tom Fleming.
Music: Muir Mathieson. *Production manager*: Pamela Paulet.   (24 mins.)

A PRIDE OF ISLANDS (1973)
Production: Ogam Films. *Direction*: Oscar Marzaroli. *Photography*: Martin Singleton.
Treatment and commentary: Alan Campbell McLean. Commentary spoken by John
Young. *Editing*: Brian Crumlish. Music composed by Frank Spedding, conducted by
Marcus Dods.   (31 mins.)

THE PRIME OF MISS JEAN BRODIE (1968)
Production: 20th Century-Fox. *Producer*: Robert Fryer. *Direction*: Ronald Neame.
Screenplay by Jay Presson Allen, adapted from the novel by Muriel Spark.
Photography: Ted Moore. *Editing*: Norman Savage. *Production designer*: John Howell.
Music: Rod McKuen, directed by Arthur Greenslade.
With Maggie Smith, Robert Stephens, Pamela Franklin, Gordon Jackson, Celia
Johnson, Diane Grayson, Jane Carr, Shirley Steedman, Lavina Lang, Antoinette
Biggerstaff, Margo Cunningham, Isla Cameron, Rona Anderson, Ann Way, Molly
Weir, Helena Gloag, John Dunbar, Heather Seymour, Lesley Patterson.   (116 mins.)

PROSPECT FOR A CITY (1967)
Production: Campbell Harper Films. *Direction*: Henry Cooper. *Script and
commentary*: Colin McWilliam. *Narration*: Tom Fleming. *Photography*: Mark
Littlewood, assisted by Allan Armstrong. Music arranged and conducted by
Eric Roberts and played by the Pro Arte Orchestra of Edinburgh.
Produced to commemorate the bi-centenary of Craig's Plan for the New Town of
Edinburgh.   (25 mins.)

RED ENSIGN (1934)
Production: Gaumont-British. *Producer*: Jerome Jackson. *Direction*: Michael Powell.
Script: Michael Powell, Jeroma Jackson. *Additional dialogue*: L. du Garde Peach.
Photography: Leslie Rowson. *Art direction*: Alfred Junge.
With Leslie Banks, Carol Goodner, Frank Vosper, Alfred Drayton, Donald Calthorp,
Allan Jeayes, Campbell Gullan, Percy Parsons, Fewlass Llewllyn, Henry Oscar, John
Laurie.   (69 mins.)

RESTLESS NATIVES (1985)
Production: Oxford Film Company, in association with Thorn EMI Screen Enter-
tainment. *Executive producer*: Mark Bentley. *Producer*: Rick Stevenson. *Associate
producer*: Paddy Higson. *Direction*: Michael Hoffman. *Screenplay*: Ninian Dunnett.
Photography: Oliver Stapleton. *Photography*: Michael Coulter. *Editing*: Sean Barton.
Music: Stuart Adamson, performed by Big Country.

Filmography

With Vincent Friell, Joe Mullaney, Teri Lally, Ned Beatty, Robert Urquhart, Bernard Hill, Anne Scott-Jones, Rachel Boyd, Iain McColl, Mel Smith, Bryan Forbes, Nanette Newman. (89 mins.)

RING OF BRIGHT WATER (1969)
Production: Palomar. *Producer*: Joseph Strick. *Direction*: Jack Couffer. *Screenplay*: Jack Couffer and Bill Travers, based on the book by Gavin Maxwell. *Editing*: Reginald Mills. *Photography*: Wolfgang Suschitzky. Music composed and conducted by Frank Cordell. *Art director*: Ken Ryan. *Wildlife consultants*: Hubert Wells, Tom and Mabel Beecham.
With Bill Travers, Virginia McKenna, Peter Jeffrey, Roddy Macmillan, Jameson Clark, Jean Taylor-Smith, Helena Gloag, W. H. D. Joss, Archie Duncan, Kevin Collins, John Young, James Gibson, Michael O'Halloran, Philip McCall. (107 mins.)

ROB ROY (1953)
Production: Walt Disney Productions. *Producer*: Perce Pearce. *Direction*: Harold French. *Screenplay*: Lawrence E. Watkin. *Photography*: Guy Green. *Editing*: Geoffrey Foot. *Art direction*: Geoffrey Drake. *Music*: Cedric Thorpe Davie.
With Richard Todd, Glynis Johns, James Robertson-Justice, Michael Gough, Finlay Currie, Jean Taylor-Smith, Geoffrey Keen, Archie Duncan, Marjorie Fielding, Eric Pohlmann, Ina de la Haye. (81 mins.)

RULER OF THE SEAS (1939)
Production: Paramount. *Direction*: Frank Lloyd.
With Will Fyffe, Douglas Fairbanks Jr., Margaret Lockwood. (96 mins.)

SCOTCH MYTHS (1982)
Production: Everallin. *Producer*: Barbara Grigor. *Script and direction*: Murray Grigor. *Photography*: Mark Littlewood. *Animation*: Donald Holwill. *Music*: Ron Geesin.
With Samuel Fuller, Chic Murray, John Bett, Juliet Cadzow, Walter Carr, Robbie Coltrane, Ron Geesin, Sorel Johnson, Alex Norton, Bill Paterson, Freddie Boardley, Brian Pettifer, David Rintoul, Finlay Welsh. (95 mins.)

SEAN CONNERY'S EDINBURGH (1982)
Production: Viz. *Producer*: Lynda Myles. Written and directed by Murray Grigor. *Photography*: Mark Littlewood.
With Sean Connery. (30 mins.)

SEAWARDS THE GREAT SHIPS (1961)
Production: Templar Film Studios. *Direction*: Hilary Harris. From an outline treatment by John Grierson. Commentary written by Clifford Hanley and spoken by Bryden Murdoch. Music composed by Iain Hamilton and conducted by Marcus Dods. Animation by James Macaulay. (29 mins.)

A SENSE OF FREEDOM (1981)
Production: Scottish Television. *Direction*: John Mackenzie. *Script*: Peter McDougall.

Photography: Chris Menges. *Editing*: Alan Macmillan. Music composed by Frankie Miller and played by Rory Gallagher and his band.
With David Hayman, Alex Norton, Jake D'Arcy, Sean Scanlon, John Murtagh, Roy Hanlon, Fulton Mackay, Martin Black, Hector Nicol, Frank Welshman, Katy Gardiner, Billy Jeffrey, David Steuart. (105 mins.)

THE SHEPHERDS OF BERNERAY (1981)
A film by Allen Moore and Jack Shea. Conceived, produced and recorded by Jack Shea. Photographed and edited by Allen Moore. (56 mins.)

SING OF THE BORDER (1964)
Production: British Transport Films. *Producer*: Edgar Anstey. *Direction*: Tony Thompson (completed by Kenneth Fairbairn and Muir Mathieson). *Photography*: Trevor Roe. *Editing*: Ian Woolf. *Music*: Muir Mathieson. *Singers*: Ian Wallace, Constance Mullay, Lisa Turner, Rory McEwen.
Commentary written by Tony Thompson and spoken by Muir Mathieson.
(20 mins)

A SONG FOR PRINCE CHARLIE (1959)
Production: Anvil Films (Scotland). *Producer*: Ralph May. *Direction*: Hans Nieter. *Sound supervisor*: Ken Cameron. *Photography*: Adrian Jeakins and Walter Lassally. *Editor*: Bill Freeman. *Unit manager*: Pamela Paulet. *Music director*: Edwin Astley. *Commentary*: James Cameron. *Narration*: Duncan McIntyre. Songs by the Edinburgh University Singers conducted by Herrick Bunney. (18 mins.)

THE SPY IN BLACK (1939)
A London Films Production, presented by Alexander Korda. *Producer*: Irving Asher. *Direction*: Michael Powell. *Screenplay*: Emeric Pressburger, from Roland Pertwee's adaptation of a novel by J. Storer Clouston. *Photography*: Bernard Browne. *Editing*: Hugh Stewart. *Production designer*: Vincent Korda. *Music*: Miklos Rozsa, directed by Muir Mathieson.
With Conrad Veidt, Valerie Hobson, Sebastian Shaw, Marius Goring, June Duprez, Athole Stewart, Agnes Laughlin, Helen Haye, Cyril Raymond, Hay Petrie, Grant Sutherland, Robert Rendel, Mary Morris, George Summers, Torin Thatcher, Bernard Miles. (82 mins)

SQUADRON 992 (1940)
Production: GPO Film Unit. *Direction*: Harry Watt. *Photography*: Jonah Jones. *Music*: Walter Leigh. (20 mins.)

STORM IN A TEACUP (1937)
A Victor Saville Production. *Direction*: Victor Saville and Ian Dalrymple. From the play by Bruno Frank, adapted by James Bridie.
With Rex Harrison, Sara Allgood, Cecil Parker, Vivien Leigh, Gus McNaughton, Ursula Jeans. (87 mins.)

Filmography

THAT SINKING FEELING (1979)
Production: Minor Miracle Film Co-operative. *Direction and screenplay*: Bill Forsyth.
Photography: Michael Coulter. *Editing*: John Gow. *Art direction*: Adrienne Atkinson.
Music: Colin Tully and Sydney Devine, performed by Colin Tully, Alan Taylor,
Martin McManus, Kenny McDonald.
With Tom Mannion, Eddie Burt, Richard Demarco, Alex Mackenzie, Margaret
Adams, Kim Masterson, Danny Benson, Robert Buchanan, Drew Burns, Gerry
Clark, Anne Graham, Billy Greenlees, John Hughes, Eric Joseph, Alan Love, Derek
Millar, Margaret McTear, James Ramsey, Janette Rankin, Douglas Sannachin.
(92 mins.)

THE THIRTY-NINE STEPS (1935)
Production: Gaumont-British. *Producer*: Michael Balcon. *Assistant producer*: Ivor
Montagu. *Adaptation*: Charles Bennett, from the novel by John Buchan.
Continuity: Alma Reville. *Dialogue*: Ian Hay. *Photography*: Bernard Knowles. *Art
direction*: Oscar Werndorff. *Editing*: D. N. Twist. *Music*: Louis Levy.
With Robert Donat, Madeleine Carroll, Lucie Mannheim, Godfrey Tearle, John Laurie,
Peggy Ashcroft, Helen Haye, Frank Cellier, Wylie Watson. (87 mins.)

THE THIRTY-NINE STEPS (1960)
A Betty E. Box-Ralph Thomas Production. *Producer*: Betty E. Box. *Direction: Ralph
Thomas*. *Screenplay*: Frank Harvey from John Buchan's novel. *Photography*: Ernest
Steward. *Art direction*: Maurice Carter. *Music*: Clifton Parker.
With Kenneth More, Taina Elg, Barry Jones, James Hayter, Michael Goodliffe, Duncan
Lamont, Brenda de Banzie, Reginald Beckwith, Faith Brook. (93 mins)

THREE SCOTTISH PAINTERS (1963)
Production: Templar Film Studios. *Producer*: R. A. Riddell-Black. *Direction*: Laurence
Henson. From a treatment by James Cumming. *Photography*: Gordon Coull.
Commentary spoken by John Shedden. (22 mins.)

TROUBLE IN THE GLEN (1954)
Production: Republic Studios. *Producers*: Herbert Wilcox and Herbert J. Yates.
Direction: Herbert Wilcox. Screenplay by Frank S. Nugent, from the novel by
Maurice Walsh.
With Margaret Lockwood, Orson Welles, Forrest Tucker, Victor McLaglen, John
McCallum, Albert Chevalier, Janet Barrow, Eddie Byrne, Ann Gudrun, Moultrie
Kelsall, Margaret McCourt, Alex McCrindle, Duncan McIntyre, Jack Stewart.
(91 mins.)

TUNES OF GLORY (1960)
Production: Knightsbridge. *Producer*: Colin Lesslie. *Direction*: Ronald Neame. *Screen-
play*: James Kennaway. *Photography*: Arthur Ibbetson. *Editing*: Anne V. Coates. *Art
direction*: Wilfred Shingleton.
With Alec Guinness, John Mills, Dennis Price, Gordon Jackson, John Fraser, Kay
Walsh, Susannah York, Duncan Macrae, Alan Cuthbertson. (107 mins.)

VENUS PETER (1989)
Production: British Film Institute, in association with Channel Four Television, Scottish Film Production Fund, Orkney Islands Council and British Screen. *Producer*: Christopher Young. Direction: Ian Sellar. Written by Ian Sellar and Christopher Rush. *Photography*: Gabriel Beristain. *Music*: Jonathan Dove. *Editing*: David Speirs.
With Ray McAnally, David Hayman, Sinead Cusack, Gordon Strachan, Caroline Paterson, Juliet Cadzow, Sheila Keith, Peter Caffrey and the people of Stromness and the Orkney Islands. (94 mins)

WAVERLEY STEPS (1947)
Production: Green Park Unit of Verity Films. *Direction*: John Eldridge. *Screenplay*: John Sommerfield. *Photography*: Martin Curtis. (30 mins.)

WEALTH OF A NATION (1938)
Production: Film Centre. *Producer*: Stuart Legg. *Direction*: Donald Alexander. *Photography*: Harry Rignold and Jo Jago.
Commentary written by Donald Alexander and spoken by Harry Watt. (18 mins.)

WEDDING GROUP (1933)
Production: Fox-British. *Direction*: Alex Bryce.
With Alastair Sim, Fay Compton, Barbara Greene, Patrick Knowles, Ethel Glendinning, Bruce Seton, Michael Wilding. (69 mins.)

WESTERN ISLES (1942)
Production: Merton Park Studios. *Direction*: Terence Egan Bishop. *Photography*: Jack Cardiff. Commentary spoken by Joseph McLeod. (15 mins.)

WHISKY GALORE! (1948)
Production: Ealing Studios. *Producer*: Monja Danischewsky. *Direction*: Alexander Mackendrick. *Screenplay*: Compton Mackenzie and Angus Macphail, from the novel by Compton Mackenzie. *Photography*: Gerald Gibbs. *Music*: Ernest Irving.
With Basil Radford, Joan Greenwood, James Robertson-Justice, Gordon Jackson, Duncan Macrae, Compton Mackenzie, Jean Cadell, A. E. Matthews. (82 mins.)

THE WICKER MAN (1973)
Production: British Lion. *Producer*: Peter Snell. *Direction*: Robin Hardy. *Screenplay*: Anthony Shaffer. *Photography*: Harry Waxman. *Editing*: Eric Boyd-Perkins. *Art direction*: Seamus Flannery. *Music*: Paul Giovanni.
With Edward Woodward, Britt Ekland, Diane Cilento, Ingrid Pitt, Christopher Lee, Lesley Mackie, Walter Carr, Irene Sunters, Lindsay Kemp, Ian Campbell, Russell Waters. (86 mins.)

Filmography

WILD HIGHLANDS (1961)
Production: British Transport Films. *Producer*: Edgar Anstey. *Associate producer*: John Legard. *Direction*: Ian Ferguson. *Photography*: Ronald Craigen and John Buxton. *Editing*: John Legard. *Music*: Edward Williams.
Commentary written by Harry Green and spoken by Stephen Murray.   (21 mins.)

YOU'RE ONLY YOUNG TWICE (1952)
Production: Group 3. *Executive Producer*: John Grierson. *Direction*: Terence Egan Bishop. From the Play, *What Say They?*, by James Bridie.
With Duncan Macrae, Charles Hawtrey, Patrick Barr, Joseph Tomelty, Robert Urquhart, Ronnie Corbett.   (80 mins.)

Bibliography and Principal Sources

1. **Through Myth to Reality (pp. 1 – 8)**
    Alan Jay Lerner. *The Street Where I Live*. (London. Hodder & Stoughton. 1978).
    Angus Calder. 'Piercing the Shroud of Scott's Myths'. *The Scotsman*. September 28, 1987.
    John Grierson. 'The Projection of Scotland'. *The Spectator*. May 6, 1928.
    John Grierson. 'I think the best amateur film I ever saw was *The Singing Street*. It was in some ways technically terrible but it was wonderful to me and quite unforgettable. I never think of it without feeling that mere skill can be a waste of God's good time. The reason for it being wonderful was quite simple. Somebody loved something and conveyed it'. BBC Scotland's *Arts Review*. April 3, 1955.
    Ian Macpherson. 'Filmy Caledonia'. *Glasgow Herald*. April, 1941.

2. **From *Annie Laurie* to the Glourie (pp. 9 – 30)**
    Review of *Annie Laurie*. *Today's Cinema*. May, 1927.
    Lillian Gish. *The Movies, Mr. Griffith and Me*. (London. Columbus Books. 1988).
    Michael Powell. *200,000 Feet on Foula*. (London. Faber & Faber. 1938). *A Life in Movies*. (London. Heineman. 1986).
    Kevin Gough-Yates (Ed.) *Michael Powell in collaboration with Emeric Pressburger*. (London. British Film Institute. 1970).
    William Rothman. *The Murderous Gaze*. (Cambridge, Massachusetts. Harvard University Press. 1982).
    Anne Edwards, *Katharine Hepburn: A Biography* (London, Hodder and Stoughton, 1986)
    John Grierson. Review of *Said O'Reilly to McNab*. *World Film News*. September, 1938.
    Will Fyffe. Interviewed by Thomas Baird. *World Film News*. October, 1938.

3. **The Debt to *Drifters* (pp. 31 – 48)**
    John Grierson. *Grierson on Documentary*. Forsyth Hardy (Ed.). (London. Collins. 1946. Faber & Faber. 1966. University of California Press. 1966. Abridged edition. Faber & Faber. 1979).
    W. H. Auden. 'Night Mail'. General Post Office.
    Harry Watt. *Don't Look at the Camera*. (London. Elek Books. 1934).
    The first Films of Scotland Committee, 1938-1943. Chairman: Sir Gilbert

Bibliography and Principal Sources

Archer. Members included George Donald, John Grierson, Neil Gunn, Alex. B. King, O. H. Mavor, Charles Oakley, William Quin, W. Dickson Scott, George Singleton, Sir John Sutherland, The Hon. John Weir, Norman Wilson. The films were *The Children's Story, The Face of Scotland, Scotland for Fitness, Sea Food, Sport in Scotland, They Made the Land, Wealth of a Nation*; and, later, *Dundee*. The first seven films had 4,725 showings in British cinemas, the audience total conservatively estimated at 22,491,000.

Ritchie Calder. 'Scottish Testament'. *World Film News*. 1937.

4. The War Years (pp. 49 – 60)

Forsyth Hardy. *Films of Scotland*. (Edinburgh. HMSO. 1948).

Harry Watt. *Don't Look at the Camera.*

Richard Winnington. Review of *Waverley Steps. News Chronicle*. August 23, 1948.

5. Knowing Where to Go (pp. 61 – 79)

Michael Powell. *A Life in Movies.*

L. A. G. Strong. *The Brothers*. (London. Gollancz. 1932).

Neil Gunn. *The Silver Darlings*. (London. Faber & Faber. 1941).

Monja Danischewsky. *White Russian, Red Face*. (London. Gollancz. 1966).

G. W. Stonier (William Whitebait). Review of *Whisky Galore! New Statesman*. June 25, 1948.

Michael Korda, *Charmed Lives*. (London. Allen Lane. 1980).

6. Adapted from the Novel (pp. 80 – 100)

Scott Mackie. Review of *The Gorbals Story. The Scots Review*. November, 1950.

Review of *What Say They?* (as a play). *Glasgow Herald* London theatre critic. Quoted by Winifred Bannister in *James Bridie and His Theatre*. (London. Rockcliff).

Dilys Powell. Review of *The Brave Don't Cry. The Sunday Times*. October 24, 1952.

Bosley Crowther. Review of *The Brave Don't Cry. New York Times*. November 6, 1952.

Neil Paterson. *And Delilah*. Short Stories including *Scotch Settlement*. (London. Hodder & Stoughton. 1951).

7. Scottish Office Moves Half Way (pp. 101 – 140)

The second Films of Scotland Committee. Original membership: Chairman: Sir Alex B. King. Hon. Teasurer: Hugh Fraser. Members: Robert Clark, Hugh Cowan-Douglas, W. Dickson Scott, Frank Donachy, J. B. Frizell, John Grierson, John Gibson Kerr, Tom Honeyman, J. Douglas Hood, W. C. Kirkwood, Sir Robert Bruce Lockhart, Sir David Lowe, Sir John Mactaggart, Bart., James Maxwell, Robert Neilson, Charles A. Oakley, Neil Paterson, William Quin,

J. W. Rodger, George Singleton, Norman Wilson. Membership when the organisation ceased trading: Hon. President: George Singleton. Chairman: Andrew Stewart. Members: Donald Alexander, James S. Christie, Alex Clark, Emilio Coia, John A. Donachy, Professor T. A. Dunn, James M. Dinwiddie, Professor Sir Robert Grieve, F. M. Irons, J. Gibson Kerr, John Lindsay, Charles MacGregor, R. B. Macluskie, Jean Morton, C. A. Oakley, Ken J. Peters, J. K. S. Poole, Ronald V. Singleton, Oliver C. W. Thomson, Lord Wallace of Campsie, William Wallace (Hon. Treasurer), R. A. Williamson, Norman Wilson. Neil Paterson (Consultant). James Wilson (Director).

John Grierson. Treatment for *Seawards the Great Ships*. Edinburgh Film Festival programme. 1958.

John Chittock. *The Financial Times*. January 6, 1976.

John Grierson. Review of *The Land of Robert Burns*. *The Living Cinema*: International Film Quarterly. Spring, 1957.

8. After *Brigadoon* (pp. 141 – 170)

Penelope Houston. 'Orson Welles'. *Cinema: A Critical Dictionary*. (London: Secker & Warburg. 1980)

Ingrid Bergman. *Ingrid Bergman: My Story*. (London. Michael Joseph. 1980).

Ephraim Katz. *The International Film Encyclopaedia*. (London. Macmillan. 1979).

Dylan Thomas. *The Doctor and the Devils*. (London. Dent. 1953).

David Newport. 'The Doctor and the Devils'. *Screen International*. Feb. 16, 1985.

Walter Elliot. *Long Distance*. (London. Constable. 1943).

Monja Danischewsky. *White Russian, Red Face*.

Trevor Royal. *James and Jim: a Biography of James Kennaway*. (Edinburgh. Mainstream. 1983).

9. Two Bills and Some Others (pp. 171 – 208)

Philip French. *The Observer*. January 4, 1979.

Liz Taylor. Interview with Bill Forsyth. *Scotsman* colour magazine. 1981.

Alan Brien. Review of *Gregory's Girl*. *The Sunday Times*. June 14, 1981.

Allan Hunter, Mark Astaire. *Local Hero: The Making of the Film*. (Edinburgh. Polygon Books. 1983).

Victoria Mather. Review of *Housekeeping*. *The Daily Telegraph*. December 3, 1987.

Dr T. C. Smout. On the Clearances. *A History of the Scottish People, 1560-1830*. (London. Collins. 1969).

Nancy Banks Smith. On *The Cheviot, the Stag and the Black Black Oil*. *The Guardian*. June 7, 1974.

Jimmy Boyle. On *A Sense of Freedom*.

Jessie Kesson. *Another Time, Another Place*.

Iain Johnstone. Review of *Restless Natives*. *The Sunday Times*. June 30, 1985.

Paul Scott. Letter in *The Scotsman* on *Scotch Myths*. January 6, 1983.

10. A Will to the Future (pp. 209 – 215)

John Grierson. 'By our Doorstep'. *John Grierson's Scotland*. Forsyth Hardy (Ed.) (Edinburgh. Ramsay Head Press. 1979).

John Grierson. 'The Relationship between the Political Power and the Cinema'. Celebrity Lecture. Edinburgh International Film Festival. August 24, 1968.

Index

Index

Index

Index

List of Plates